MOUNTAIN BREEZE

traversing the Indian landscape

A Travelogue.

SAURAV RANJAN DATTA

Live Simple. Live Simplicité.
Email: livesimplicite@ gmail.com

Mountain Breeze – Traversing the Indian Landscape.
Copyright © 2024, Saurav Ranjan Datta.
A Simplicité Initiative – 2024.

Co-Published By Qurate Books Pvt. Ltd.

ISBN: 978-93-5898-693-8

Typeset at Minion Pro, Garamond & Times New Roman.
By Shubham Singh, Team Simplicité.

CONTENTS

Preface

Most often in our lives, travelling feels like an elixir. Although, we must have heard that cliché a million times, it is a reality for many people. There are folks who have shunned the materialistic life altogether and have taken the road to salvation. In India, there are mendicants, monks, and sadhus for whom travelling is the only invigorating way to sustain an otherwise rough life. The roads are their places of dwelling, their homes. Even many ordinary citizens who are not hermits can maintain a life of solitude amidst the urban cacophony by travelling solo. After all, where else can one gulp some nectar so spiritually and physiologically enriching than in places under the shade of a matronly nature? In the following lines of a poem by William Wordsworth, we can sense its underlying meaning:

> *'I wandered lonely as a cloud*
> *That floats on high o'er vales and hills,*
> *When all at once I saw a crowd,*
> *A host, of golden daffodils;*
> *Beside the lake, beneath the trees,*
> *Fluttering and dancing in the breeze.'*

In simple terms, nothing gives us as much soul-fulfilling happiness as exploring a new place does. The sheer joy of walking amidst the verdant greens of a new land is always refreshing. To many, the thrill of new sights and sounds feels blissful. Travelling has not only given us abundant joy but has improved our lives in many ways. Personally speaking, it has done wonders for me. Let me tell you my story in a few words. To start with, I was brought up in one of the remotest corners of India. Being from a middle-class simple family, I was also quite shy in my teens. It was a very small town where I lived; quiet in those days, with lots of open space. The quaint nature of that place gave us poise and a silent equilibrium of the cerebrums. The town has taught us many things. It gave us an everlasting urge to embrace nature wherever we go. The borough also piqued our interest in remaining amidst nature's verdure and respecting it in all its ethereal forms. However, there was a flip side to it too. Often, in those days, we would shun company and retire to the confines of our family. Some people might take that as self-centeredness or a lack of self-assertiveness. But in today's time, not being able to communicate with people of all kinds may hurt you in serious tangible terms. That will be more so if you are a part of the big, bad corporate world of a developing nation. However, things changed when I started travelling. Once on the road, you have to speak to strangers, meet new people, experience new customs, and learn all kinds of new things. Those valuable experiences, in turn, not only made me affable but also street smart. In addition, travelling gave me enough materials to observe and learn in the process, experience new things, and thus develop some lifelong enriching habits. Travelling has also made me aware of the significance of environmental conservation and ecological balance, hitherto unknown to an average student like me. Ever since I started touring as a passion some time back, my outlook on life has taken a completely different direction. My opinion of this world and towards the surrounding environment has also changed for the better. Let me also add here the fact that travelling can be of various types. However, the first thing that any tourist must always consider is their responsibility towards the environment of a new place and its culture and people. There should be serious efforts made or steps taken to maintain the sanctity of a place. One must never litter a site in any way. In addition, it is of utmost importance to abandon plastics or any other environmentally degradable items before visiting any ecologically sensitive zone. Since this book is an attempt to bring out the beauty of this country from the point of view of a common person, we need to emphasise the environmental issues and solutions more than anything else. But rest assured, this book is not about any technical jargon related to the above subject, but a pure travelogue full of stories, anecdotes, and tips. Let us always strive to make ourselves environmentally responsible wherever we travel. Since this work is about places related to mountains and hills, we may commence our journey with a few lines from a famous Emily Dickinson poem:

> *'The mountain sat upon the plain*
> *In his eternal chair,*
> *His observation omnifold,*
> *His inquest everywhere.'*

One

INTRODUCTION

"Suhanaa safar aur yeh mausam hasin,"
"Hamey dar hai ham khona jaaye kahi."

When these lines from an old song were broadcast into our drawing rooms via Door Darshan and Chitrahar in the late 1980s (when television became a common fixture in most Indian households), it created a spell in the minds of every child in my vicinity. The inherent melody in that number reverberated in our ears with its soulful rendition ad nauseam. On the other hand, the song's video simply astounded us with its outdoor imagery amidst nature. If you check that song on YouTube now, you will find that the piece features a young and handsome Dilip Kumar Saab, once a matinee idol of the Hindi film industry. The song's video shows him roaming around the exquisite countryside of some part of this country. Hence, the tune as well as the tapestry of the background in that video lingered in our minds for a long time during those tender years.

But before we proceed here, let us, first of all, explain the song to people who are not aware of Hindi cinema or its language. The above two lines can be roughly translated into English as,

"What a lovely journey in such pleasant weather."
I am just worried about being lost here forever.'

This song is a part of the Bimol Roy-directed movie "Madhumati", released in the year 1958. (I mentioned the nineteen-eighties above because that was the time when I started watching television). It was sung by the inimitable Mukeshji, and the music was composed by the legendary Salil Chowdhury. A quick search on the internet will reveal to you that they did the initial shooting of this movie in the mountains of the Kumaoni Himalayas (in current-day Uttarakhand state). However, the technicians later shifted the shooting to the Western Ghats because they could not capture the initial part of the shooting clearly on their cameras. Those shots probably appeared hazy when seen by naked eyes later on. However, this song is not our topic for the day today. It was just a preamble to bring your kind attention to the subject of this work – the incredible landscape of this country called India. To explain it further, this song was one of the first known instances that developed in many of us, at least the kids of my generation, an urge to imitate Dilip Saab in it. That is to roam around a beautiful valley like him with gay abundance, yodelling a tune while taking in the fresh sights and sounds of the breath-taking landscapes all around us. Personally speaking, the song still haunts me today, although I may not listen to it as regularly as I used to once upon a time.

Now, let us come to the next part of our journey. Now, we have to select the kind of landscape we would like to discuss here. Of course, we are taking into account only the incredible vistas of our mountains and vales in this piece. However, let us remember that India as a country is so vast that it is just not possible to cover many of its beautiful spots within the scope of one book. To tell you the truth, leave alone a single volume, even a series might not suffice for this kind of work. Hence, we have chosen our spots quite randomly but specifically the places where yours truly has personally visited. However, the theme of this book is strictly about those spots that one can explore only while hiking. But before going into the details, we need to explain the differences between hiking and trekking or mountaineering. According to the definition of the Oxford English Dictionary, hiking means the activity of going out for long walks around the countryside for pleasure. Under the strictest meaning of this definition, hiking means anything that is not very strenuous and has no specific parameter of any minimum distance covered. But, that is my interpretation, to be honest. In the real sense, hiking encompasses everything, be it trekking, backpacking, or long walks. On the other hand, only professionals can undertake the task of mountaineering. That is because one needs a certain amount of training along with some level of physical conditioning to compete in the sport of mountaineering. Yes, we may also consider mountaineering as one of the extreme sports. The other name for mountaineering is alpinism, and there is an international federation of alpine bodies, duly recognised by the IOC.

Trekking, on the other hand, is divided into several categories nowadays. Most of the agencies that conduct trekking expeditions divide their journeys into the classifications of easy, moderate, and difficult trekking adventures. According to those divisions, there are probably different preparations for each and certain required physical conditioning. Nevertheless, we are not discussing the technical aspect of an alpinist's know-how here or the places where people can go only after much preparation. Yet, everybody must remember one cardinal rule about travelling in the mountains (or hills) of any country. One needs to have some minimum physical fitness and certain levels of energy and enthusiasm to undertake such endeavours. A traveller must undergo some cardio exercises before embarking on any place situated in the mountains of India (or anywhere).

As we mentioned above, the places and journeys discussed in this book are purely for hiking. Some are a bit strenuous, but in no way could they be categorised as serious trekking expeditions. Some of these spots are offbeat destinations, and some are quite popular. But there is one thing common between all of them; they are some of the most beautiful places in India without any doubt.

In the meantime, before we proceed further, there are certain other things that we need to discuss first. As we know, the word "mountain" is a very generic term. Again, according to the Oxford dictionary, one of the meanings of a mountain is: 'a very high hill or a natural elevation that is quite notable for its high altitude.' In India, the term "mountain" invariably conjures up the image of the Himalayas in everybody's minds. But the Himalayas are not the only mountains in India, and neither are the stories here only about Himalayan vicinities. India encompasses many ranges of this geographical feature. Broadly speaking, the hills, for that matter, can also be considered under the generic title of mountains, since one is just the smaller type of the bigger one. Though technical definitions may differ, all of the hilly nooks and crannies will be discussed in this book under the category of mountain vistas.

The continent of Asia has some of the highest mountain ranges on this planet – the Himalayan range, Hindu Kush, Karakoram, Pamir, Kunlun, Altai, Zagros, etc. (I am taking these names randomly and not as per the highest or the longest). Out of them, the Himalayan range is the most popular one, as it houses the topmost peaks on this planet. The Himalayan range traverses multiple countries and hence has always been very important politically. The Himalayas also cover a huge part of my country, from the northern Ladakh-Kashmir to the extreme east of North Eastern India. The Himalayas are generally divided into the categories of the Greater Himalayas, the Lesser or Middle Himalayas, and the Shivalik or Outer Himalayas. There are many sub-categories too. For example, the North-Eastern states of India are part of the Purvanchal range (the altitude is not very high there), which is considered an extension of the Himalayas on the Eastern side. We also categorise the state of Uttarakhand into two distinct Himalayan zones in general terms – the Garhwal Himalayas (where we have hill stations like Mussoorie, Dhanaulti, etc.) and the Kumaon Himalayas (with hill stations like Nainital, Ranikhet, Almora, etc.). The Himalayas undoubtedly have some of the most beautiful and stunning vistas of nature. Yet, India has other mountain ranges too. They may not match up to the massiveness of the Himalayan range or its altitudinal superiority. But most of them have equally, or sometimes even more, breathtakingly beautiful spots, sans the snow. On the other hand, the Himalayan peaks, for that matter, are spots of perpetual snow.

The oldest mountain range in India is the Aravali, covering many states in the North and West of this country. People must have heard about the hill station of Mount Abu in the state of Rajasthan. Mount Abu is a part of the Aravali. Simultaneously, some other famous mountain ranges of India are the Western Ghats, the Eastern Ghats, Satpura, etc.

Let me mention here that my personal favourite amongst them is the Western Ghats. This beautiful mountain range runs parallel to the Western Coast of India. Though it is not as high as the Himalayas, the Western Ghats are one of the most important zones on this planet for biodiversity and natural splendour. The other name for this range is the Sahyadri Mountains. It is also one of the UNESCO World Heritage Sites in India in the natural category. Just imagine this; the Western Coast of India already has some of the best beaches in Asia. Together with them, when you find mountains as you move up a bit towards inland, it becomes an occasion for travelling regularly to this zone.

The Western Ghats run from the state of Gujarat to the beautiful environs of Kerala, while plying through Maharashtra, Goa, and Karnataka, and also include the Nilgiri Mountains of Tamil Nadu. The range is responsible for many rivers and climatic conditions like monsoons, etc. It also has gaps, discontinuities, and meeting points with other highlands. Again, this range is too important to be covered within the scope of a single volume. However, it is sufficient to say that its integral part, the Nilgiri Mountain range, has been a favourite zone with many film-makers in India. Film crews have shot numerous movies in its nooks and corners. Since this range has some of the most beautiful spots in India, there is no dearth of visitors travelling to it all year round. Some of the places in the Nilgiri feel just like heaven. You can trust this writer on that. In addition, while visiting there, one can easily identify certain shooting locations that he or she might have seen previously in their favourite movies.

Simultaneously, the Eastern Coast of India has the Eastern Ghats Mountains, or hills, running parallel to it. Apart from that, there are other ranges too. In this regard, we must mention here two important parallel highland ranges that run through the mid-section of India. They are called the Satpura and the Vindhya. These two ranges through Central India have divided the sub-continent into the Northern Indo-Gangetic plains and the Southern Deccan Plateau.

At the end of the day, all these highland beauties have given India a unique diversity in terms of its geography and climate that is not often witnessed in any other part of this world. India is vast and its topography is varied. That is why conservation has become an utmost priority now. India is not truly its real self without its mountains and hills. In this compendium, we shall now traverse the various ranges and see for ourselves how unique each place is. These mountains are not only sublime in their variety of biodiversity. They are also hotbeds for the intermingling of many things – the local people, their unique hospitality, the cuisine, the culture, the faith, and innocence. Many experts might shake their heads at this clichéd romanticising of our mountains. But then what is wrong with all that? After all, if you truly love something, the chances are that you will also care for it. So, with a joyful ballad in our hearts forever, let us now start our *suhanaa safar*.

Two

THE ABODE OF DEVI'S

CEREBRUM

Once, there was a lake on the top of this mountain. Soon, the lake got dry and the villagers were unable to gather water from it. Therefore, in due course of time, they started to call it by its name. In the local language, a dry or empty space means 'kaana', and the term for a pond or lake is always 'taal.' Hence the name of this place came to be known as 'Kaanataal' or 'Kanatal' This place is that perfect proverbial "sleepy hamlet" that travellers so often search for and later cherish in the lap of the Himalayas. In November two thousand and twenty-one, when the global pandemic abated a bit, yours truly made a journey to this place. For the record, the Garhwal Himalayas of the state of Uttarakhand are the location of this little paradise. As mentioned earlier, we generally divide this state into two distinct zones: Garhwal and Kumaon. We must remember here again that both these regions house some of the most beautiful tourist destinations in this country. Uttarakhand is also a place of immense religious importance for the faith of Hinduism. Some of the most sacred and pious places of worship of the Hindu deities are located in this state, in its Himalayan valleys and peaks. It is not without reason that we reverentially call this state by the epithet of "Devbhumi." This term more or less means 'The Land of the Gods' (or the 'Abode of the Gods'). The etymology of the name Uttarakhand is also simple. It just signifies 'Northern Land or Northern Region or State'. We broadly call the people of the Garhwal section Garhwalis (and the Kumaon people Kumaonis). You can trust this author on this one; the local Garhwalis are some of the most good-natured, broad-minded, incredibly hospitable folks that one can come across in this country. Their congeniality and helpful attitude are almost legendary now. The etymology of the name Garhwal is also very interesting. Anywhere in India since time immemorial, the term "Garh" usually means a fort or a fortified enclosure. In the same way, there is a term called "Wala" that is mostly used as a suffix here with other names and words. This suffix signifies ownership of something. In earlier times, during the mediaeval ages, there lived a local king in this region, probably by the name of Ajaypal. That monarch brought several forts or enclosures in this mountainous zone under his sway. So, the principality thus formed came to be identified strongly with him. Therefore, the name that he acquired because of this was "Garhwala" (Lord of the forts). In this way, this region eventually came to be known as Garhwal, a stretch of beautiful places and equally beautiful people.

"Sir, thoda chai peeney chaale?" (Sir, shall we have some tea now?) This request came from my driver after we had driven for about an hour from the Dehradun Airport on the way to our destination. By that time, we had left the plains and the towering mountains all around us had also started to make themselves visible to my timid eyes. We eventually got off after another half an hour. Our car came to a bend in the road where we found a few roadside tea stalls on the edge of the deep gorge. The windows of the car had remained closed all this while, so I did

not realise how cold it had become outside by that time with the change in our elevation. A gust of unadulterated pure mountain air hit my face with its chilly numbness, the moment when I came out of my vehicle. But the vista beyond the tea stalls towards the valley enraptured a special chord in my bosom. I kept on staring at the scene without blinking, with a cup of hot steaming tea in my hands. At the same time, the sun kept on casting its rays tepidly as it slowly withdrew itself behind the horizon. There was a melancholy calm all around. Melancholy but not agony; a touch of tired sadness giving way to a blissful evening. By that time, my jarred city-bones and urban nervous system had also started cooling down, with the inherent tranquillity all around us.

Let us, for the record, remember here that after getting off from the Dehradun Airport, we took the Narendranagar Road, bypassing the evergreen Rishikesh. We have to mention here that the Dehradun Airport has a unique name. It is called the Jolly Grant. Nowhere in India would you come across such a name. The majority of aerodromes in this country are named after local public officials or famous national leaders. From this airport, once you travel via the Narendranagar Bypass, reaching up to Chamba, Kanatal, Danaulti, and Mussoorie one by one until you come down again to the Dehradun Airport, this entire journey would feel like an arc. Geographically, this entire route traverses like a circle, and the roads are fantastic here, except when the snowfall starts or during monsoon. During that period, the pathway can become treacherous or inaccessible, depending on the amount of snowfall, which can be heavy at times (or the landslides happening due to heavy rains). Once, towards the start of this millennium, when yours truly was a college student in the Doon Valley, we went for a road trip along this route. We drove our motorbikes on one fine Sunday morning in January of that year, traversing this aforementioned zone. But unfortunately, we received heavy snowfall on our way and remained stranded for many hours in the middle of nowhere. Our perilous sojourn ended, thankfully, when the snowfall receded towards the evening. God must have blessed us at that moment, as we were finally able to come back safely to our homes that night.

Nonetheless, as mentioned above, this time it was November and the chances of snow were as feeble as some of the gentle mountain streams. (That turned out to be quite true during the entire course of my stay). The goal of this trip was to stay at Kanatal and explore some of the places around it, especially the pious Hindu pilgrimage centre of Surkhanda Devi Temple. Before I went there, many people had informed me that this temple, together with its location, is one of the most beautiful spots in Uttarakhand.

The Temple of Surkhanda Devi is not just another Hindu mandir. It has great religious significance as well as a cultural heritage. According to Hindu mythology, one of the supreme Gods of our Holy Trinity is Lord Shiva. The others are Lord Vishnu and Lord Brahma. We have many names for Lord Shiva – Mahadeva, Rudra, Shivshambhu, Shankar, and several others. During the Puranic (ancient) times, Lord Shiva's wife was Goddess Sati, who was the daughter of King Daksha. Daksha himself was the son of Lord Brahma, who created him through the power of his mind. As the story goes, Daksha never liked his daughter's husband, since Shiva followed an ascetic lifestyle and dwelled amongst several kinds of vagrants. After all, who would like their son-in-law to be a homeless monk? Therefore, once, when Daksha performed an important yajna (fire sacrifice), he did not invite either his daughter or her husband. Sati was a pious and dignified wife who could not take such an insult to her husband. Since she felt humiliated and hurt, in her rage, she jumped into that sacrificial fire and self-immolated herself in the process. As that tragedy unfolded, Lord Shiva came to know of it immediately. He was a caring husband and loved his wife with all his heart. Her loss was too much for him. Being a God of cosmic destruction, Lord Shiva, then in total sorrow, took the body of Sati on his shoulders and started his all-pervasive Natarajan destruction dance. He vowed to demolish the entire creation till the time Sati's body had not completely melted away. As his dance started, the entire universe came into tumultuous chaos. Fearing the consequences, the other gods then rushed to Lord Vishnu and implored him to save everybody. Lord Vishnu's most potent weapon is the 'Sudarshana Chakra,' a lethal discus of considerable power. In the hope of pacifying Mahadeva, Lord Vishnu then went after Natarajan wherever his dance took him away. In the meantime, Lord Vishnu also used his chakra to cut down the dead body of the Goddess. Therefore, wherever a part of Devi Sati's body fell after being severed by the discus, that place became a pilgrimage centre according to our legend. Those pilgrimage centres are now known in the Indian sub-continent as the "Shakti Peethas." The roughly translated English form of this term is' The Pious Abode of the All-powerful Holy Mother Goddess.' According to the same legend, Devi Sati would later go on to be reincarnated as Devi Parvati.

The above tale is ubiquitous in this country. We have been hearing it since we were toddlers. The Shakti Peetha shrines are mentioned in many of our Puranas, which are some of the most important canonical works from the total gamut of the Holy Scriptures of Hinduism. However, according to them, the number of Shakti Peethas differs as per a particular work. Nevertheless, it is sufficient to say that in India, we have many Shakti Peethas. Some are also found in Bangladesh, Nepal, and Pakistan, as per the general belief. The Temple of Devi Surkhanda is one of the Shakti Peethas. As per the common understanding, the most important part of the physiology of a human being or divinity, the head along with its brain, of Devi Sati fell on that spot where Surkhanda Devi Temple stands today. Hence the name too, if you think closely. The name of Surkhanda Devi is a corruption of the word 'Sirkhanda', which roughly means 'the part of the severed head.' That was how this temple got its name, in all probability, and also the reason for its being so important to the people of this faith. Many devotees travel there in the hope of getting blessings from the Divine Mother. But not only the religious part; this temple is also important and a sight to behold for other reasons. We shall see that in the next few paragraphs.

Hence, when I travelled there and reached Kanatal at around 8 pm that day (as mentioned above) after travelling for almost four hours from the Jolly Grant Airport, my excitement was quite palpable. As I was ushered in by my host for the trip, Mr. Ramola, into his resort, the cold outside felt numbing to the core for a traveller from the plains. Kanatal is located at an elevation of around 8500 feet above sea level, which is higher than any other well-known hill station. But even then, I found a group of young men (probably from Punjab) making a bonfire under the open sky on that night. They did it right outside my cottage in that extreme cold and kept on dancing and drinking till the wee hours of the night. To be honest, their joviality and unadulterated cheerfulness also assured me. *"If I go out this night, the cold at least won't kill me."* That was the thought that kept lingering in my mind then.

The next day started with much excitement. By the time I was up, the sun was already beating down its gentle rays over every nook and peak in that vicinity. The morning felt like a new world, brandishing everlasting charm and happiness. The weather was nippy but jolly at the same time. The cold had covered itself altogether in the Himalayan Sun by then, a phenomenon that is only visible between two everlasting lovers in the classic stories. Together, they felt like a loving quilt made by a caring Mother Nature. As we drove off after a heavy breakfast, a serenity descended upon this troubled urban soul. The same driver-chap from the last day took me to the base of the Surkhanda Devi trek, a few kilometres away from my Kanatal residence. Let me mention here now, that from the road, the temple is almost a 3 km steep trek upwards. The trekking path is quite narrow and the ascent is not easy at all. The steepness is like a straightened-up thin ladder with several bends. (At the time of the writing of this piece, the construction of a ropeway cable car was underway in that place to take people easily to the top. This would help the old people who wish to visit that shrine. But in the meantime, it's an uphill task to climb that path).

The moment we reached the base, my driver-chap did a volte-face and declined to join me on that trek. *"Saabji, it's too strenuous for me." You go, I will wait here.* A few moments of cajoling and coaxing him did no good, and I had to take the road eventually all by myself. The base of the Surkhanda Devi trek is like a market with all kinds of shops looking after the needs of the devotees. During my visit, we found some religious flags embossed with numerous symbols fluttering in the wind. These gave the air in that vicinity quite an elating sanctimonious feel in comparison to the other places on that route. The temple is perhaps the highest point in that stretch. Now, let me inform you here that once you hike up a bit on that road, there are also horses available to take you up if you cannot walk or if the uphill climb becomes too tiring. But even riding a horse on that narrow stretch could be a gut-wrenching experience. Your heart might come to your mouth. But quite surprisingly and to my utter astonishment, I found many Garhwali couples on that road who could not only easily walk that entire distance by foot. But they were even carrying their children on their shoulders while hiking up. At some point, unable to suppress my curiosity, I asked a young father and mother how they could easily do that. *"Bhaisaab, hum yaha barbar aate hain. Bhakti main bahut hi Shakti hai."* *(Brother, we come here all the time. There is great strength in faith and devotion).*

Well, coming back to our story, please take note that once you reach that temple, one has to put off his or her shoes outside. Devotees can then enter the shrine after washing their hands. (Washing hands should be mandatory before entering any place of worship. During my journey, I found that the temple was open to all; people from any country could visit that place).

The temple of Devi Surkhanda is one of the finest specimens of exemplary traditional Pahari Himalayan architecture that a tourist can witness in this country. The structures are so exquisite that the whole architecture feels like the creation of divinity themselves, who might have descended upon this mortal realm once just to create this particular place of worship. As you move around that complex, a mood of serenity is sure to brush you with an infinite calm and an urge to know the universal soul more deeply. The sides of this temple complex have such incredible views of the Himalayan peaks that hitherto any mountain lover would not have witnessed them so close at arm's length, in all their phantasmagorical glories.

Personally speaking, after reaching there and after offering my prayers to the Goddess, the whole environment made me go into a trance. I was looking at the other visitors without actually looking at them at all. The Himalayan peaks in the distance kept on shining under that mild but glowing sun of an Indian winter. While time was always at a premium when on a short trip, the mood was effervescent and not a moment passed when returning to my base felt like a sense of sadness. One could stay there forever, under the auspicious eyes of divinity, under the care of the universal Mother Goddess. Coming back to regular life after a visit to that place felt like a throbbing melancholy. The view of the entire universe from that temple elevation of around 9000 plus feet above sea level felt quite breath-taking to my eager eyes. But then, as that Robert Frost poem goes, *"But I have promised to keep, and miles to go before I sleep, and miles to go before I sleep."*

For that reason, the descent to the base was soon made. Upon reaching the road below, I was unable to find my driver at first. But in hindsight, that also gave me the chance to taste other local cuisines. This time, I tried a more modest Garhwali meal at an unpretentious food outlet, which I found to be situated on one side of that road. The traditional '*thali*' was too tasty and, trust this author, that food experience was not an exaggeration at all (a claim made after gourmet tasting adventures of many years). Soon after that, as my driver-chap came back, the moment also appeared to say goodbye to that place. But the memories of the Surkhanda Devi Temple complex journey have stayed in my heart ever since that day. What a place! What a beautiful place!

(Note: Just to add, while in Kanatal, one must also not miss exploring the deep jungles of Kaudia Forest. That green area is an experience in itself, especially for hikers and trekkers.)

Three

THE TEMPORARY CHAMBERS OF THE PANDAVAS

If you ever happen to visit India, there is one thing that will never escape your notice. Any tourist would find it hard to miss this phenomenon of places being intrinsically connected to their local myths or folklore. Either the name of an Indian city or the story of its creation has invariably had a Mahabharata or a Ramayana connection. These two epics are so ubiquitous in the lives of every Indian that a day seldom passes here without their mention or invocation,

We have seen the importance of faith in our last chapter. We have also seen how religion is palpable in the lives of every citizen of this land. Many places in this country have numerous divine origin stories. As a matter of fact, a number of people here believe that the deities have created those places all by themselves. Sometimes, the common person attaches a character from the epics of Ramayana and Mahabharata with the creation of a place or a geographical feature, or their etymological origin. (For example, the Bhimbhetka Rock Shelters near Bhopal got their name from the common belief that the second Pandava brother from the Mahabharata, Bhim, used to sit there when resting). These stories are part of the common faith. We are not doubting their origins in this chapter nor debating their historical authenticity. Whatever might have happened or not happened, these tales reign supreme in the hearts of many, and have been instrumental in formulating the cultural heritage of this sub-continent.

The state of Madhya Pradesh is one of the largest provinces of India and is located centrally in this country, far away from the borders on all sides. The state name here itself signifies the interpretation of 'Middle/Central Region.' This state is extremely important for its rich history, geology, biodiversity, and tourism. One of its cultural contributions is the lending of the name of Gondwanaland to a presumed erstwhile supercontinent. According to the continental drift theory, experts imagine that this supercontinent of Gondwanaland was formed during the Neoproterozoic period of Earth's geological history. The name was derived from the Gond tribe, which inhabited (and still inhabits) a region corresponding to the modern state of Madhya Pradesh, as well as some other areas of the adjoining states. The history behind the naming of this presumed supercontinent is quite lengthy and the subject of a separate study. But it is sufficient to say, as proposed by several experts, that the supercontinent's name came into popular culture due to this theory, explained in the following lines: During earlier times, a part of Central India was commonly known as Gondwana because of that tribal group's presence. Hence, when the Europeans explored Central India, they found some rock formations there that they thought were of the most ancient types in this sub-continent. Once they assumed that those stones of the Gondwana region originated from an earlier landmass, the naming of that supercontinent became inevitable after that.

However, the state of Madhya Pradesh is not only important for its geology and history, but also for its massive biodiversity and natural beauty. One of the most beautiful places in this state is the hill station of Pachmarhi. This town is a part of the Satpura Range, as discussed earlier, and forms an important administrative part of the Satpura Biosphere Reserve. Thankfully, Pachmarhi is still an offbeat destination in the pan-Indian tourism circuit. That is why the place has retained its vibrant nature and a pure air bereft of any urban cacophony. Though the elevation of this hill station is not much (roughly a mere 3500 feet above sea level), the place makes up for that with its eerily silent aura and rustic effervescence. The entire region here is green-carpeted with an abundance of verdure and feels like an innocent utopia.

The history of Pachmarhi is also very rich. Once, this region saw the might of Queen Durgavati, a brave warrior who gave a valiant fight against the army of the mighty Mughal Emperor Akbar. In the historical sense, Madhya Pradesh as a zone has always been famous for its female luminaries. It has also witnessed the bravery of Queen Avantibai, who fought the British forces just like a tigress, the several Begums of Bhopal, Rani Ahilya Bai Holkar, and many others like them.

As we revert back to our topic, let us assert here that none of us can deny in any way the contribution of the British towards the development of Pachmarhi. As a matter of fact, most of the hill stations in India today have a distinct British legacy. Our colonial masters developed these places because they just couldn't bear the terrible heat of the Indian plains during those summer months. Also, the hill station climate reminded them of Good Old Blighty. In the same way, a British military officer by the name of Captain James Forsyth once found this place (i.e., Pachmarhi) and established a centre here. That is why the town is still an army cantonment today. Also, it is not without reason that the people of Madhya Pradesh call it "Satpura Ki Rani" (The Queen of the Satpura Range). The quaint charm of the place when Captain Forsyth founded it around the middle of the nineteenth century has retained its old magic to this day.

Now, we come to the most important part of this chapter. The places that one can visit while in Pachmarhi There are spots in this hill station that can only be covered while hiking. But there are also numerous places where a motor vehicle can take you easily. But before venturing into those, we must talk about the legendary backstory of this place, as alluded to above. The name Pachmarhi comes from a mythological connection. As per the local language, *'pach'* means five, and the word *'marhi'* roughly means 'caves'. Therefore, it is believed that the five Pandava brothers from the epic "Mahabharata" came here during their exile and built those caves to reside in for that time being. If you go there now, you will find that those rock-cut caves are currently the most famous tourist destination in this place. The caves are located atop a small hill, and one has to hike up a bit to reach them. There is also nice landscaping done around its entry point. In reality, those caves must have been carved out either by Buddhist or Jaina monks during ancient times. This is true of most of the rock-cut cave structures of India.

Not only are the tales of the Pandavas associated with the name of this hill station itself, but there are also other spots here that have equally interesting mythological backstories. One of the most popular destinations in Pachmarhi is Handi Khoh. This viewpoint is a deep gorge covered in dense herbage. The vegetation of this narrow and steep valley is so thick that the base is not visible under the cover of a massive jungle. According to legend, this gorge was once a lake where a malicious serpent lived. In his rage, Lord Shiva, one of our trinities, then one day burned that serpent. But the resultant heat even dried the lake, and now it looks like a cooking pot. The local word for a cooking pot is *handi*, and hence the name. It is quite interesting to note that some of the foliage found in this valley is akin to that generally found near any water body. Nevertheless, there are several other legends like this in Pachmarhi.

Before the savage pandemic of COVID-19 hit us in India in the year 2020, a couple of us made a trip to this hill station in October 2019. At that time, we had no inkling of this dreaded pandemic that was to change our lives forever. Travel was smooth and life was so carefree. From my home city of Kolkata, we took a flight to Nagpur in Maharashtra. From that city onwards, it is a five-hour drive to Pachmarhi. One can also go to Pachmarhi via the state capital of Bhopal. But from there too, the drive still takes around four hours of your precious time. However, both drives are worth the effort. We found the roads well laid out and clean and green. Once in Pachmarhi, MP Tourism has numerous budget accommodations that one can avail of for their stays. We stayed in a beautiful bungalow with ample open space and acres of green all around us to relax and chill. When we reached there around 9 pm, we could not make out the immediate beauty of the place. It was dark, and we found that there were not enough streetlights present to illuminate the town. As a consequence, the next morning gave us a pleasant surprise when our driver took us to the nook and cranny of this place. Let me explain a bit now why Pachmarhi is a different hill station than the rest. For one thing, the roads are quite flat there and there are no steep climbs like in any other Indian hill station. Also, being a cantonment area, the town is exceedingly clean and the green canopy is ubiquitous. Wherever you go in Pachmarhi, it is always green all around you. The centre of the town has a small market and almost no crowd presence like any other congested Indian city.

Since the idea of this book is to cover only those places that are only accessible through hiking, we shall now discuss those beautiful spots of Pachmarhi that we experienced while walking under the autumnal sun of that year.

For the start, we had specifically instructed our driver to take us to those places first where we could trek a bit. As for the other easy spots, we scheduled them for a later date. Accordingly, the driver-chap took us to an area called Reechgarh. From the road where he dropped us off, we started our walk through a thick jungle. As we slowly made our way, the place felt very calm, with only the buzzing of some unknown insects from the nearby thickets. The path was rocky for us at that moment, but a peaceful mood descended upon everybody during the trek. Soon, we came near a massive rock formation that resulted in some caves and passages. As we braved the slippery boulders there to get down inside those pathways, it gave us quite an adventure. From that cave formation, the backyard opens up to a beautiful valley with dense jungle for miles and beyond. We walked through that only to find ourselves getting lost in the process. Hence, we had to retreat from that area, which should be attempted only with a proper guide. We soon learned the etymology of the Reechgarh caves, which felt eerily prehistoric. According to the local people, these caves were once the dwelling abode of numerous sloth bears (Oh! God!). The local word for a bear is Reech, thus the name.

Once back to the main road, the driver then took us to another very famous destination in this town, the Jatashankar Caves. While in Pachmarhi, the Jatashankar Caves should not be missed. It's a wonderful site with massive cave formations made of giant boulders and a pious silence always residing inside those holy cavities. Legend has it that Lord Shiva kept himself hidden in this place once. The name Jatashankar itself means the matted locks of Lord Shiva. Upon reaching there, we had to walk quite a bit from the spot where our driver parked the car, up to the entrance of this complex. Then we had to go down a lot using the built steps to reach the cave. (So, it was quite strenuous while climbing up on our way back). Inside the cave, we found a gentle stream flowing and a couple of monks sitting quietly beside it. As we paid our respects to the deity, we came out and sat outside for a long time, taking the quietness all around us into our jarred nerves. We came back eventually, as we had other places to cover.

Simultaneously, we were then driven to another religious shrine. The visit there started with another cave temple, popularly called the 'Bade Mahadev.' Again, there is a mythological tale connected to this shrine too. It is said that right here, an Asura (demon) by the name of Bhasmasur was tricked and eventually killed by Lord Vishnu, another of the trinities of Hinduism. From there, a short hike of around a mile took us to Gupt Mahadev, a cave shrine so narrow that anybody fat or bulky would not be able to enter that place. Another two and a half kilometres from the Gupt Mahadev Shrine would have taken us to the Chauragarh Peak and Temple, but by that time, our energy had given way to exhaustion. So, we backtracked and came back to our resort. The next day took us on some easy trips, but that story is for some other day.

Let me now add a few important points here. Pachmarhi has ample sites of natural interest for visiting tourists that would be hard to cover in one single trip. Not only are there incredible cave formations or rock-cut structures, but the place also has some amazing waterfalls. But one has to go down and up quite a bit to reach the base of those waterfalls. Therefore, some level of fitness is necessary. The town is also extremely green, as discussed earlier, but it has hardly any happening places like pubs or bars. So, people who love parties or event-related entertainment won't find anything there after sunset. This place is strictly for people who love silence, greenery, and solitude. One should also care for the sanctity of this place while visiting because any use of plastics there would naturally harm its environment. People should also respect the silence of the jungles while in Pachmarhi. At the end of the day, we can safely conclude that Pachmarhi is one of the best hill stations in India in every sense of the term.

Four

THE ABODE OF THE LEOPARDS

The wind outside kept on howling with unhinged fury. At the same time, in my small room at the homestay, I kept on shivering. The cold was unlike anything I'd ever felt before. That morning, I had reached this small hamlet of Chatakpur, perched atop an elevation of almost 8000 feet above sea level. But the cold was numbing, probably because the village is part of the famous Senchal Wildlife Sanctuary, and I found it covered in dense foliage. The month was April, in the year 2017. At that time, the furious sun of the Indian summer was scorching the plains of this land with its unabashed anger. It was exceedingly hot then, if I could remember properly. So, I took a short break from my office and travelled to this place. But what awaited me was an experience of a lifetime.

As expected, the first night in a new place would always turn out to be difficult for me. I had this bad habit of not being able to sleep properly in a new place during those years. (A malady I have rectified now). Therefore, during that night in Chatakpur, especially with the cold added, I could hardly sleep. As I kept on turning the sides, the night became deep and the cold pinching. After much struggle, I got up at midnight to go to the toilet. When I came back, something pushed me to open the windows and take a look outside. An action that I regretted later. Before that, let me tell you that the homestay that I had selected in that hill station was situated right beside a cliff. From there, one could see the lush green downward slope giving way to a verdant valley covered in tea plants. Therefore, my windows had a wide view but were visible only during daylight. At that moment, as I tried to make meaning of the outside darkness from my aperture, I saw a white something just a few feet away, right on the edge of that cliff. Before I could react, the thing jumped from that rim and vanished into the thin air. A sound of anguish akin to a cry came out of my mouth, only to be drowned by the outside gale. The window shutters were bolted in no time. As I turned towards the bed, my shivering increased many folds, which felt like apoplexy at that moment. For a few seconds, my head also felt fuzzy. *"What was that? Did I see that?"* The confusion remained as I remembered that during the same day, while on my flight, I had read a few Ruskin Bond ghost stories. Now, I might have over-imagined the outside window thing, clearly the aftermath of reading those stories. But in any case, sleep kept eluding me for the rest of that night.

As I got up in the morning, the sun was already blazing. The entire room emanated a happy glow. A view of the dense foliage outside with a friendly sun (what a change!) beating down upon them felt like an unspoilt garden of a fairyland. That also reminded me that I had a trek planned for that day. A hike through the rugged Senchal Wildlife Sanctuary till the Tiger Hill of Darjeeling; a trail of around 25 km in totality to and fro; a distance calculated as per the local people. When I got ready, the homemade breakfast also awaited me with a palpable fine fragrance. While munching on those delicacies, I informed my host, Mr. Thapa, cursorily about what I had seen the previous night. That amiable gentleman turned grave at my mention of the incident and noticeably evaded the topic. Hence, for my part, I did not press the matter further. After all, I was there for just two nights. By that time, my guide for the day appeared. The guy was only a teenager, hardly 17 or 18 years old. I was quite astonished to see such a young lad as my guide. But he seemed quite confident. Upon asking, we learnt that his name was Tashi. He looked shy but was a strong lad.

We embarked on our journey at around 8 am. Both of us took a backpack each, with water, energy drinks, and some other small items. As we skirted the village gate to take the path towards the jungle, right at that moment, on our right-hand side, the Kanchenjunga peak appeared in all its resplendent glory. We stopped for the time being and brought our hands to our foreheads as a mark of respect to that eternal shining monk. The mountain looked like a white meadow, painted with the colours of a yellow flame. The view was mesmerising as ever. But we had to leave soon on our errand.

That being the case, we initially took the paved path that carried us from the village gate towards the open country. Thus, after walking for a few kilometres, around a bend on our left through a clearing, Tashi entered the forest, followed by me. Therefore, finally, we made an entry into the kingdom of green. By that time, Tashi, with his long legs and supple frame, dashed for it, but I had to remind him not to hurry. After all, he had a middle-aged fat guy from the plains to guide him through that meadow. Henceforth, we trudged ahead at a slow pace, taking in the aura of the surrounding flora. In that moment of exploration, what I found was just an enormous assemblage of trees of different kinds. The foliage looked so lush that its long shadows exuded a childlike softness. The weather, in the meantime, had turned misty, with gentle fog caressing the tree-tops. The resultant atmosphere made the surroundings mysterious, but with the caring touch of a fine fabric. For the initial hike, the path was quite bumpy. We had to go up and down several times, braving the steep rises and the gradual downward slopes. But soon the trail became even and sometimes the sun made a peekaboo appearance in our eyes. After about an hour, we came to an undulating valley. Tashi told me to stop and rest there for some time. So, we sat down and took our water bottles out for an energy sip. In the meantime, my young guide switched to his mobile phone, which had no network, but he played some already downloaded songs from it. To my utter surprise, I found Pink Floyd's numbers emanating from that phone. (Successful globalisation!).

As I looked around and observed the surrounding scenario, I found the valley right out of a picture book. It looked mind-blowing, with the wild grass gently swaying to the Himalayan zephyr. The horizon appeared to have been lost in that unending green. Sometimes the tall trees, but at other times the different coloured bushes, came to our eyes. Was it the Garden of Eden, which was so romanticised in our childhood stories? What if I stayed there forever? Several conflicting musings of that kind kept on dancing in my mind. But my young guide soon got up, and I had to follow him at his insistence. As both of us surged ahead, we traversed exciting terrain amidst the sounds of numerous birds, unheard by a man of the urban plains. Tashi kept on talking about his family and his daily life. After about another couple of hours, we came to the base of Tiger Hill. Soon, we left the jungle and got up onto the metallic road towards the hill summit. But the Tiger Hill viewing platform was overcrowded by then, we found to our dismay. I had no intention of joining that cacophony. So, we stopped and found a roadside tea stall to rest at, just beside a beautiful temple. Upon paying, the tea stall served us hot, steaming tea and some tasty masala

Maggies. After refreshing ourselves, we went to that temple to offer our prayers. I found the temple eerily quiet but beautiful and, upon enquiring, learnt its popular name - Sinchal Devi Mandir. What a beautiful moment it was, my mind refreshed by the atmosphere of the place as my body remained tired after a long hike. But as time was limited, the moments saw both me and Tashi taking the trail again to return to our village. Since the path was more or less the same for the entire distance, the return trek would not have been downhill. We assumed that it would take the same amount of time. But by that time, my walking pace had also been increased, as returning by nightfall was a priority. On our return journey, we did not stop at all but just slowed down whenever we had to take a sip from our water bottles. Tashi told me about the Senchal Lake and suggested a diversion to visit it. But I was too eager to return and so I skipped the attraction for the time being. As our steps got us closer and closer to the village, the shadows started to grow longer. The evening was fast approaching.

When we thought that the village was just a few kilometres ahead, the darkness became imminent. It was only a matter of a few minutes then. At that moment, a sharp bend on the road came. As we skirted and took the turn to the other side, a flash of yellow crossed that path like lightning only a few metres ahead of us. The thing was gone before we could gauge the head or tail of its features. Tashi grasped my hand tightly and motioned me to stop. He also put his fingers in his mouth, signalling me not to make any sound. But the movement of his lips told me it was a leopard. We stood there still like a pyramid for many moments. I shivered all that time. Honestly, my nerves were already jarred by last night's vision. It was too much for me to take at that second. Hence, the moment Tashi said, *"Let's Go,"* I sprinted like Usain Bolt. All this while, I was the one who was unable to keep up the speed with my young guide. But from that moment on, Tashi just couldn't match my pace. A kind of superhuman strength came to my bones. I ran as if chased by a mighty serpent. Before long, the paved road came into view from where we had started and then the dim lights of Chatakpur. People there had already started making their dinner, it seemed. A sigh, the sign of a sense of relief, came out of my mouth. Tashi also sat down beside the village gate upon reaching it to take a breath. But my mood, by that time, had become jubilant. Not only had I completed an arduous trek that I could boast about on social media (lol!), but an unexpected danger was also averted in the process. The heart emanated joy and some melancholy at the same time. My departure from that beautiful place was scheduled for the next day. Goodbye, O Himalaya, till next time.

Now, it is time to discuss the facts about that place and the journey. Chatakpur is a beautiful eco-village situated not far from Darjeeling. It is a part of the Senchal Wildlife Sanctuary, as you can observe from the above narration. Senchal is one of the oldest wildlife sanctuaries in India and possesses a plethora of flora and fauna. The description of that natural vista requires the genius of a Bibhutibabu to justify its sublimity. (Note: The Bengali author, Shri Bibhutibhusan Bandopadhyay, has left an indelible mark on the cultural landscape of this country. His narration of nature and wildlife reads like a celestial piece of prose, perhaps composed by a supernatural being. His entire body of literature is just extremely soothing). From yours truly, you can take this assurance that the journey to Chatakpur and the subsequent stay there will be most invigorating and physically refreshing. The green canopy of the village is mind-boggling, and visitors will be surprised to see so much foliage making such a dense presence in that place. Chatakpur has many jungle trails other than the hiking route narrated above. One of the most popular trails there is a small hike to a place called Pokhri. Pokhri is actually the local word for a pond. This short-distance forest trek will take you to a body of water inside the jungle, where the local people also perform their religious rites on its banks. Also, for people who are engaged in the profession (or hobby) of birding, this small hamlet is an ideal spot. The entire village periphery there is nestled amidst so much green that one can easily come across numerous birds, depending upon the time and season.

Chatakpur also has many viewpoints from where the entire surroundings appear sublime. The peak of Kanchenjunga is easily visible from these points when the weather is right. My suggestion for the Senchal trek is to travel there with a group. The sanctuary has too much wildlife. The place can get quite dangerous for just two people. One can check the local newspapers of that region, which report from time to time about various incidents of tourist importance. Like the often loitering of Himalayan Black Bears seen near the Tiger Hill Temple or in other places of this sanctuary. Hence the advisory above. For the record, the name "Tiger Hill" does not mean that this hilltop houses many tigers. The etymological origin of this hill is not clear to us yet. Just like the current name, it could have been anything. But why Tiger? We have no idea. In any case, a thorough research on the etymological background of all the names of places there is most definitely required. But coming back to the topic of Chatakpur again, this hamlet is always worth a visit. However, do check the current rules and regulations of any place before you make your plan. If one can brave the extreme cold, the best time for visiting any hill station in the Eastern Himalayas is any month other than the monsoon season.

Five

WHERE THE LORD APPEARED FROM A COW'S EAR

The time has come now for us to travel from the Eastern Himalayan splendour to the Western coast of India. We shall discuss a place situated in one of the southern states of India, and unique with its highland vistas, leafy terrain, and unhindered sea gale. As alluded to earlier, India has no dearth of natural wonders. There are destinations here that can give any intrepid traveller the experience of a mountainous vista and a sea breeze at the same time. If you think that is impossible, well, think again and explore to find it for yourself.

Gokarna is a small town in the north of Karnataka state. In this sub-continent, Karnataka is one of the most prosperous provinces. The capital city of Bangalore (Bengaluru locally) is known as the Silicon Valley of India. From this capital city, Gokarna is around 500 km away. The town of Gokarna is indeed a sleepy place. Sometimes the place feels more like a prosperous large village than the category of a town. But that is not important. Once you drive from Bangalore or any nearby city like Mangalore, Udupi, or from any place in Goa to this borough, you are entering a zone of unadulterated natural wonders. For your information, the Dabolim Airport in Goa is the nearest air link (at the time of writing this piece) to this place. When a tourist's car leaves the highway and takes the interior roads towards Gokarna, the surroundings there feel like a perfect rural setting. Here, a note must be made regarding an old habit of 'yours truly'. From my youth, the rural South of India always held a special place in our hearts. We grew up reading and later watching Malgudi Days. The stories of RK Narayan felt like the tales of our own lives. Therefore, it is not without reason that Mr. Narayan's place as a writer can only be considered amongst the highest echelons of human genius. As a result, ever since then, whenever I have travelled to South India, the scent of coffee beans in my nostrils and the search for a Malgudi-like town with those characters have also journeyed with me.

Therefore, in the year 2017, when I made a trip to Gokarna, the drive through those interior roads just before reaching the coastal town transported me back again to the reminiscences of those youthful stories. But before we proceed further on this journey, a short description of Gokarna as a tourist destination is needed in this context.

The name 'Gokarna' simply means the ear of a cow. One would wonder about the strangeness of this name. But this is a place intrinsically connected to Hinduism. As a matter of fact, this entire zone is connected to one of the trinities of Hinduism – Lord Shiva. In the main town of Gokarna, the Mahabaleshwar Temple is an embodiment of the presence of God in his Atmalinga form there. In addition, not far from this coastal abode is the Murudeshwar Temple, another very holy place blessed by Lord Shiva. Therefore, the legend behind the naming of Gokarna also feels natural. It is said that here in this very place, Lord Shiva once surfaced in his bodily form from the ears of a cow. In Hinduism, a cow is often seen as an embodiment of

Mother Earth. Therefore, it is quite understandable that this place exemplifies the human story of Genesis. The Supreme God appearing as a child from the womb of the Mother Goddess is actually the story of creation, where a mother gives birth to her son and life takes its form. What a beautiful allegorical representation that this place teaches us. As a result, Gokarna, religiously as well as spiritually, is one of the most important centres of Hinduism.

On the other hand, geographically, this place takes the shape of an ear as the two rivers of Aghanashini and Gangavali gleefully embrace its contours. From the main town towards the north, the attractions of this place lie one after the other towards the south. There are five main beaches in Gokarna, most of them flanked by the beautiful highlands of the Western Ghats. As we move south from the main town, which houses the main Gokarna Beach, we come across one by one, the Kudle Beach, Om Beach, Half-Moon Beach, and Paradise Beach. These beaches run from North to South, one after another, as stated above. When I travelled to this place, the accommodation was arranged at one of the decent motels, situated on a cliff above Kudle Beach. From there, the Kudle Beach area looked just like the shape of an English C to my eyes. When my car gradually came to the valleys near the coast, it was as if we were entering a hill station. The roads were covered with thick vegetation. My driver also warned me about the presence of wildlife. All around us, not a single dwelling or a dweller came to our notice during that ride. But civilisation made itself visible as we came nearer to the resort.

Let us remember again that all these four beaches of Kudle, Om, Half-Moon, and Paradise are located away from the main town and thus have become the go-to places for foreigners and hippies alike. Since these places are flanked by steep, hilly terrain and dense foliage, the serenity here can only be compared to that of a hermitage. Gokarna is indeed a place of contradictions. While the main town is an epicentre of Hinduism and thronged by multitudes of devotees, the other beaches there are paradises for hippies. While hiking in the aforementioned coves and cliffs, you would never come across any locals at any hour of the day. Well, most of the times!

One might now question the qualification of this place in a book dealing with mountainous landscapes. Here, we must draw the attention of those doubters to the famous mountainous beach trek that takes you from Kudle to Paradise beach, passing through Om and Half-Moon beaches. This trek is around 10 km one way through steep gorges and is one of the toughest for a general tourist who has scant experience of hill hiking. Of course, for professionals, it would be an easy endeavour. But the stretch takes you to so many different topographies within such a short distance that one cannot help but consider it amongst the not-so-easy highland routes for common visitors.

Let us see how. For the start, one has to walk through the dense jungles of the Western Ghats, with cliffs dropping down many feet below right onto the ocean. Then the route is narrow, steep, zigzagging, and has the frightening aspect of encountering wildlife on its way. The presence of green there is visually stunning but uncomfortable while walking, since it is thick at many path bends. On certain stretches, there are no pathways and one has to almost crawl on all four. Apart from that, the coves, the boulders, and the sudden narrow turns make this hiking a very strenuous exercise. In spite of the fact that this stretch has some of the most stunning vistas of nature, it is quite frightening to undertake.

But the experience is equally enthralling and worth the effort. On one side of the path are the steep hills of the Ghats, with their abundant verdure, and on the other side is the expanse of the blue ocean. With miles and miles of waves giving away to an infinite horizon, there is a steady flow of breeze caressing the treetops and the flowing hair of any tourist. This trek taught me one of the most valuable lessons in life. A local guide accompanied me on that trip in that year of two thousand and seventeen. That South Indian gentleman was a very modest local vendor who also doubled up as a guide in those times. When he accompanied me on that hike, I found him most amiable, gentle, and informative. But the biggest surprise was to come during the last leg of our journey. The walk from Kudle to Om felt quite easy. But things got more strenuous gradually as we neared Half-Moon Beach. Let me point out that the names of these beaches are derived from their natural shapes and sizes. For example, Om beach looks exactly like the Hindu symbol of Om when viewed from a hilltop. Same with the Half-Moon, which resembles that structure when viewed from above. Once we neared that place, I slipped and cut my ankle on the boulders. Till that moment, I had also not noticed the pathetic condition of my ever-dependent shoes. That old friend, once rugged, tough and reliable, gave way on that hike. Therefore, when I slipped, the shoes were done with and had to be thrown away. My guide, that gem of a man, that heaven-sent angel, not only lent me his sandals for the rest of that trip, he walked barefooted himself. In the process, the man braved every kind of anomaly on the road: protruding rock cones, thorns, painful stone chips, etc. Tears kept rolling down my eyes while looking at his condition. But being a weak, timid, and cowardly urban soul, I just could not help it. The size of one's heart is not dependent on the depth of his pockets. In India, in fact, the most broadminded souls are often found in the most ordinary of circumstances. While the rich and powerful here are self-centred, narrow urban mortals, the people of the hills and villages are like angels. They are like an affectionate father or mother who never cares about their own difficulties.

Now, coming back to my story, on that long hike when we finally reached the Paradise Beach, the body ached for rest and also some respite. Hence, we took a break for a couple of hours, where both of us also took a bath. That dip in the ocean refreshed our feet as well as our souls. After that, we decided to take a different route on our return journey to reach the town. By that time, my energy had been exhausted and I had no intention of testing further any of my endurance capacities. Hence, we took a jungle route this time. But as they say, where the fear is greater, untoward incidents happen quite often. On our return journey, a serpent stealthily passed by my feet, causing me to almost have a heart attack then and there. After that, thankfully, everything went smoothly, and we went back to our respective places of dwelling. My guide's name is Saaji, and if you go there today, do ask for him around the Kudle Beach. To date, I haven't found a more genuine and kind-hearted fellow like him.

The time has come now for the information part of our piece. While in Gokarna, it is not necessary to trek through those mountains to get to the Paradise Beach. During the tourist season, there are speed-boats available from Kudle to take you to those places. However, do remember that both Half-Moon and Paradise Beaches are thronged by naked hippies. Hence, the speed-boats generally don't entertain solo male visitors/stags. It is also embarrassing to take your family there, especially if you are accompanied by old guardians or parents. But leaving aside these hiccups, both beaches are like places made in heaven. Yes, they are stunning, and hence, tourists should also not litter them while visiting.

Aside from this adventurous mountain hiking, Gokarna has other options for the adventurous visitors. From this place, one can visit Murudeshwar, where the beach has many water sports. This is apart from the beautiful temple and the gigantic Lord Shiva idol there. Then, the ever popular Jog Falls is another must-visit place near Gokarna. The Mirjan Fort, Yana Rocks, etc. are some other places of interest that one can cover from this town. The beautiful coastal town of Karwar and Goa-the party capital of India, are situated to the north of Gokarna. All these places definitely make Gokarna a centre of attraction for many tourists. As a matter of fact, nowadays, many foreigners are avoiding Goa because of its excessive crowd. Gokarna has become another attractive option for them. The beauty of this place is seldom matched. The valley is extremely quiet, and the silence there soothes you instantly. But it has pitfalls too. During my visit, I found Gokarna almost bereft of places to explore after sunset. The surroundings around the Kudle cliff turned quite eerie and there were no streetlights either during that period. With the jungles all around me, my resort manager warned me against venturing too far into the darkness because of the presence of some wildlife. Hence, things became a bit boring after sundown. Though a few cafes were present then with their trance music, I found them serving pure veg cuisine to my utter disappointment. To sum it up, the silence suits the mood of that town more than other indulgences. After all, it was primarily a pious place of worship before it turned into a hippie heaven. Therefore, visiting tourists should respect the sanctity of the place at any cost. Since Gokarna is still an offbeat destination for the masses, we hope to see it remain pristine for many more years to come. Amen!

Six

STROBILANTHES KUNTHIANA'S LAND

The scent of coffee or tea is wafting around in the atmosphere and flares up your nostrils with its eclectic fragrance. The numerous mountain streams gushing from hidden coves and impeding your leisurely drive. The mystical fog emanating from the hallowed green grounds of the sleeping lady mountain. The vision of the valleys is akin to the grasslands of the Swiss Alps with their ever-friendly simple people. These are the kinds of thoughts one would come across when ruminating about Nilgiri, the Blue Mountains of South India. We have already discussed the geographical importance of this chain. But also from tourism point of view, not visiting this region would be a big miss for any wanderlust. Such is its beauty and the extent of its flora and fauna. It is not without reason that so many film units from India shoot their movies in the cosy environs of this hilly terrain.

One can call it a hill or a mountain. Nilgiri simply means "Blue Mountain" in English. One theory states that the name came to prominence because of the presence of the seasonal Nilkurinji flowers (aka Strobilanthes Kunthiana) there. The better accessibility to this region is through the city of Coimbatore.

From there, once a car takes anybody up into the hills, there are three stunning hill stations that feel like places right out of a picture book. Ooty or Udhagamandalam is ubiquitous in the collective consciousness of the Indian people, and thus it has now turned into an ugly, congested town. But the place still has some stunning spots away from the main town that could take the breath away from even the most experienced of travellers. Apart from Ooty, there are two other important places that have somehow remained in the shadows for common tourists on this route: Coonoor and Kotagiri. These two places are not as famous as Ooty at this moment (or not that popular when I visited). For people who are unwilling to take a car from Coimbatore, these places can be reached through the Nilgiri Mountain Railway, a famously created communication line from the British era. The Nilgiri Mountain Railway is a part of the UNESCO World Heritage Sites of India and can be accessed from a place called Mettupalayam in the foothills. However, please don't try to do a Shahrukh Khan like stunt on it that this filmy superstar did in the video of the song Chaiya Chaiya. For added information for the fans or non-fans of Bollywood, let me remind you here that a famous Hindi song called "Chaiya Chaiya" from a popular Hindi movie called "Dil Se" was shot here. In that song, the hero and some other actors are seen dancing on the roof of this railway. This song is available on YouTube at any time.

After the monsoon months of the year 2016, yours truly made a trip to this place. The decision to visit Nilgiri after the rains turned out to be a masterstroke. The moment the car took me through the mountains' meandering sharp bends, the cloudy, wet surroundings gave me an ethereal feeling. For people who pass through an Indian summer in one of its dusty, dirty metro cities bereft of any greenery, the monsoon is generally a common respite. The same monsoon in its moderate form can also play magic in the mountains. The vegetation turns extremely green and refreshing in our hills. That in turn also makes those places romantic with their misty mornings and foggy afternoons. The temperature drops further, and the surroundings feel like the cosy laps of ever-empathetic Indian mothers. Hence, if the rains stay moderate, not heavy, and not truant, the mountains of India after the monsoon season feel nothing less than the proverbial Garden of Eden.

The Nilgiri Mountains have no dearth of places to excite tourists. However, before we move to the theme of this piece, it is necessary to mention some of the best spots in this zone. Rest assured, a long drive from Coonoor through Ooty to the Mudumalai National Park in the plains feels heavenly. Once there, any visitor can feel the quietness and experience the abundance of that region's massive vegetation on that route. Though that journey is quite short, one way it is only two to three hours maximum, there is no dearth of excitement. Another unique experience of that trip is the temple of the once dreaded sandalwood robber, Veerappan, which is situated towards a corner of that national park. He is worshipped by the local tribes there because of his once Robin Hood-like charitable activities towards the poor villagers. Other than this drive, some of the lakes, valleys, and viewpoints of the Nilgiri Mountains feel like paradises out of this world. Special mention should be made of places like the 9th Mile Valley, Pykara Lake, Doddabetta Peak, etc. in Ooty. Whereas in Coonoor, one must not miss places like the Sim's Park, Dolphin's Nose, Lamb's Rock, etc., together with the Catherine Falls and Lord Rangaswamy Peak situated a little outside and away from that town's centre.

However, the fun is when one can walk a bit in this green zone. We have now come to the most important part of this chapter. Hence, we shall now move through the story of a place in the Nilgiri that can only be visited by undertaking strenuous trekking from the main road. When yours truly visited the area, accommodation was made in a Scottish-style old bungalow. Being situated beside the famous Sim's Park, the hotel felt not only beautiful on one hand, but also eerie because of its colonial background. However, there was (and still is) no report about any supernatural presence. The accommodation quite suited the place and also its mood. At least to me, a battered soul from the plains of Eastern India, it felt like a cosy nook. After enquiring about any trekking routes, the manager informed me of a spot called the Droog View Point, which consists of the Droog Fort. This Droog Fort has a history that might interest anybody. The great Tipu Sultan, the ruler of the erstwhile Mysore Kingdom whose bravery against the British is still remembered today, used this fort for the purpose of surveillance. He made sure to keep an eye on the surroundings by using this citadel as a watchtower for his lookouts. Today, the place is not an easy place to explore. The point is accessible only through a trek that takes a visitor through some tea gardens initially. But the hike gets difficult after a certain point in the journey. The latter path is through jungles, infested with bison and other wildlife. It is steep too, with some wonderful bends that enable astonishing views of the surrounding regions.

During my visit to this place, it was my utter good fortune to meet a very nice man as a guide. This Droog View Point should only be attempted with the assistance of an able guide. Srinivasan was his name, and he was the only one out of many, who agreed to accompany me on that trek. As we got off from our jeep in a tribal village, that I knew from Srinivasan to be the starting point of the trek, things looked quite hunky dory in the beginning. But I was to find out later on, that not all mornings often show the day. For his part, Srinivasan did warn me of the difficulty of this trek. People from the plains always found it hard, he opined.

Also, even though minuscule, the chance of meeting some not-so-congenial wildlife always existed. But I was upbeat and not to be impeded in any way. The initial stroll took us through a way, bypassing a graveyard. The inserted crosses there made me melancholy. A journey, either of life or of distances, either smooth or rough, always ends at some point, finally.

On that route, I could never gauge the distance. But the walk seemed to continue for eternity. As we moved ahead, the villagers working on the gardens reminded me of the everlasting Solitary Reaper poem by Wordsworth. And why not? We were passing through similar terrain. The breeze flowed gently while the birds sang, and the women kept on plucking the tea leaves without any cognizance of who came or went by their way. They were like sentinel beings, engaged in a meditation of their own making. Maybe they were humming some folk tunes that the wind barred us from hearing. None of them even cared to look at us, or maybe they never noticed us at all. Such was the force of their concentration. But the gardens soon gave way to jungles, and my guide became doubly conscious. On one of those steep climbs in that latter part, he showed me the Sleeping Lady Mountain, in all its resplendent and majestic shape. The peak looked exactly like a lady sleeping there in the midst of the comforting verdure. Some more stunning vistas followed as we kept on climbing. My lazy city bones by that time had started aching seriously and also objecting. But Srinivasan kept on egging me on by repeating that we had almost arrived. Oh, God! It never seemed to end and an enormous exasperation had also set in by that time in my entire being. In addition, a kind of blind fury towards my guide developed too. Damn! The guy bluffed and bluffed as the path seemed undiminishing. But he was only doing what was best for me. In the course of the day, we finally reached the Droog View Point after a long time. We found there a shabby watchtower-like structure, beset with overgrown shrubs and jungle all around. But the elevational superiority of that place enabled us to get a sweeping view of the green landscapes all around us. By that time, my legs gave away in exhaustion and as I sat down there, the sudden impact of the cold breeze with the fluttering clouds transported me into a trance like a stupor. A further walk into the surrounding jungles would have taken us to the ruins of the Droog Fort, but my guide advised me against it. There was no need to take a risk, as the surrounding views would have felt the same. But those jungles posed the danger of meeting wildlife. Hence, we refrained and stayed at the same place. As more clouds hovered and the blazing sun turned benign after some time, the afternoon was quickly turned into a dark evening. Therefore, we retreated and turned back. The return was smooth as it was downhill. By the time we reached that tribal village again, the long shadows of the impending night were almost upon us. Upon reaching the plains, we rested at a local shop and refreshed ourselves with some soft drinks and snacks. In the meantime, our jeep was also waiting for us with bated breath. As we boarded its body, the drive back to the hotel implied the end of that trip.

Certain realisations have also dawned upon me when I am reminiscing about my 2016 tour of the Nilgiri Mountains. So many things must have changed in all these years. The global pandemic must have also caused a brutal thaw in the beautiful Coonoor, Kotagiri, and Ooty region. During the lockdown, two things occurred that have again brought my attention to the Nilgiri Mountains. One, is a Hindi web series about love and betrayal that portrayed many contrasting families as protagonists living in Coonoor (though I could not identify the place at all from that TV show). Another is a heroine from the South Indian language movies, who hails from Kotagiri. In fact, she belongs to one of the indigenous tribal groups from that zone. This I discovered after becoming her fan and researching her background. But apart from all that, the place has stayed in my subconscious all this time. Sometimes, an urge even surfaces, a latent desire in the form of a question – 'Why can't we shift to that zone permanently?' After all, who wouldn't want to escape the polluted cities of India?

On a serious note, this region should be especially cared for as it is one of the most important biodiversity hotspots in India. It can be visited again once this pandemic recedes. As a matter of fact, there are only a few places in India that can truly match-up to the beauty of the Nilgiri Mountains. On that note, you can trust this scribe with closed eyes.

Seven

THE CHARM OF THE TWIN

HIMALAYAN HAMLETS

Life is so full of paradoxes and surprises. Sometimes things sound or appear exactly opposite of their intended purpose. This is especially true of India, which in itself is a country brimming with contradictions. When you roam its streets, the paradoxes come to the fore in all their quintessential forms. There are cities here that house the opulence of the privileged and, at the same time, the squalor of the unfortunate. This land has no dearth of surprises for a neophyte visitor. But it is not always to be taken from a cynical point of view. India, or Bharatvarsha, has innumerable natural wonders that are almost inexhaustible. The privilege of experiencing them makes life so wonderful here, on the other hand.

Let us now consider this. What is the image that comes to anybody's mind when thinking of the word "lava"? Surely, the picture of an extremely hot molten liquid rock coming out of a mountain opening flashes through people's minds at the mention of the above. The connotation of this very word signifies a burning sensation or mood that is often associated with a person's anger. How often do we say that a certain man or woman is angry just like burning lava? But in the eastern Indian state of West Bengal, where the eastern part of the Himalayas covers its northern fringes, that zone houses a tiny place by the same name. The hill sanctuary of "Lava," together with its twin dwelling called "Rishop" are two of the coolest places in this province. There is a demand for a separate state of Gorkhaland for this Himalayan part, but that is a part of the political history of this region. It is not a part of our subject today. The name 'Lava' must have a local meaning, which is not clear to us as yet. Rishop, on the other hand, roughly means the green top of mountains, as obvious as it can get.

Both Lava and Rishop are located quite high above the mountains. Lava has an elevation of around 7000 to 8000 feet above sea level, and Rishop is around 8,500 feet above sea level. The people of this region are mostly Lepchas and Gurkhas, two tribes that are especially known for their Himalayan associations. The Lepchas are primarily a Tibeto-Burman-speaking population. But not only due to the simplicity of these villagers here, this region has also drawn nature lovers in abundance due to its thick foliage of verdant green. There is a strange mystical aura in that vegetation. The tall trees cover the area like a green canopy of festive spirits. From the gaps in the overgrown verdure, the sun plays its own hide and seek with its gentle rays. The year was 2014, when I made a trip to this pure heaven engulfed in long shadows akin to a gothic-like presence. Both these twin hamlets of Lava and Rishop need some minimum physical stamina from the visiting mortals. Most of the trails from both these places are not easy to navigate and require some amount of hiking and trailblazing. Of course, there are readily available local guides who can help a tourist explore its nook and crannies.

The month was May, the height of the Indian summer, when I found myself sitting inside the premises of the Lava monastery one evening after reaching there from Bagdogra Airport. The road journey to that spot took about four hours after getting down from the aeroplane. But because of the steep, winding uphill roads, my petulant urban spirit got jarred by that rugged drive. Therefore, when the monastery coffee shop served me a hot steaming cup, the cold emanating from the surrounding valleys felt soothing to my bones. However, by that time, the journey up to that place had already made me accustomed to the sudden numbing drop in the temperature. The emanating fog from the depths of the surrounding gorges also transported this battered soul to his childhood days. Yes, I was chasing my naive musings. All those detective stories set against the Himalayan splendour had made me yearn to visit such a location. So, when I took the coffee cup and retraced my attention towards the exquisite architecture of the Buddhist monastery there, the visit seemed successful. The Lava Gompa was one of the finest I had witnessed at that time (and still one of the finest), and I do believe that the low-cost cafeteria still exists today under the aegis of that pious institution. Just merely sitting there, soaking in the calmness of the ambience and looking at those innocent people felt divine to this author. Those who are interested in meditation and seeking some semblance of peace in their lives must try the Lava Monastery.

That evening, as I finally and gingerly got up and went back to my hotel, the surrounding forests quickly engulfed themselves in a mysterious halo, enabled by the elongated shadows of the approaching night. I was probably overthinking, but those tall trees seemed to me like gentle sentries, observing me with their wide-awake gaze. By that time, the fog had also deepened itself and the visibility had become zero. There was nothing to do much after nightfall but retire to the hotel rooms. My host for that evening was Mr. Thapa, with whom I started chatting in the hope of passing my time.

"Sir, do you know that a great film director from your city stayed here with his cast and crew during the shoot of a movie?" Mr. Thapa asked me and, upon observing my ignorance, went on to show me the photos of that film unit. As he flipped through his album, I realised that a critically acclaimed Bengali movie was shot here. The one with a mother-daughter duo and an aged Bengali superstar from the Bombay film industry. We talked for a while till the cold became unbearable. For me, the following day was scheduled for some trekking expeditions. Mr. Thapa promised to provide me with a good guide.

As I got up with the first rays of the sunrise the next morning, my guide, Mr. Ramesh Chhetri, appeared on our doorsteps. "Sir, please hurry, we have a long day ahead." My breakfast consisted of bread toast and some juice, which did not take much time to finish. Before long, we had hit the road, and after surpassing the Lava bazaar, Rameshji entered a trail followed by me. The next few miles passed along with a myriad of emotions. My fitness came into serious question as I tried to keep up with Rameshji, huffing and putting. But at the same time, the forest took us on an otherworldly experience. Only green blossomed to our senses all around us, wherever our eyes rested. Our destination was a place called Tiffin Dara, a viewpoint to experience the Himalayan massif. In the meantime, the trail took us through dense foliage. My guide had also warned me of the presence of wildlife. But I did not bother looking at so much beauty all around me. A walk of a few tiring kilometres soon brought us to the Tiffin Dara viewpoint. But unfortunately, the clouds had gathered by that time, blocking our view. Much to our chagrin, we turned back and the downhill trek carried us to

Rishop. All through those hours, in spite of the steepness here and there, the hiking was an experience of a lifetime. No only had I the pleasure of walking through a completely dense forest, but the juxtaposition of the trees there along with the undulating nature of the land also made for an odd but pleasurable mixture. After we reached Rishop, a staple diet of hot Momos followed. From there, a jeep ride took us back to Lava. But we carried on as our next target was to hike-up the hilltops inside the Neora Valley National Park. As we proceeded towards the park's entry point, the motorable road turned rough over the boulders. The sun blazed overhead by that time as the mountain breeze followed. Upon reaching, my guide Rameshji again took me through a forested trail to a viewpoint. On that trip, I hoped to see a red panda, but the prospect eluded me. Of course, the population of that species has dwindled over the decades. When we reached the viewpoint, Rameshji pointed me to the valley over yonder, towards the horizon. The fluttering clouds were making their strong presence felt at that moment. Hence, in spite of Rameshji's sincere efforts, I could not much make out the point in the direction where the boundaries of Sikkim, Bhutan, and Bengal had met. But the views still felt alluring to my naked eyes. The mountains rolled for eternity, creating mischievous angles of natural splendour. Even the sky looked different, strongly azure as it was. The valleys and gorges, ravines and streams, and every other natural creation appeared to be the work of a meticulous mind. Not many people realise how beautiful this zone of the Eastern Himalayas is. Since most of the spots here require some physical exertion, they have remained outside the consciousness of general tourists. As we drove back to our hotel at the end of that day after the Neora Valley hike, the surroundings felt more personal. A kind of tranquil sadness filled my heart. Being from a small town, the silence of a green patch has always been more precious to me than the city cacophonies. But in such a moment, an ordinary mortal like me would always murmur those famous lines from that Robert Frost poem:

"The woods are lovely, dark and deep.
But I have promises to keep.
And miles to go before I sleep.
And miles to go before I sleep. "

As alluded to by me above, the twin hamlets of Lava and Rishop are located in the northern part of the Indian state of West Bengal. This northern part is covered by the Eastern Himalayas, and thus it is one of the most important biodiversity zones in this country. Most of the spots from these hamlets give an unhindered view of the Kanchenjunga, the third highest mountain in the world. Recently, both Lava and Rishop have also become favourite spots for people who are into birding. There are other villages in the vicinity of both these places that can be covered from there during the same trip. However, a guide must be sought while hiking the jungle trails as the region is quite infested with numerous wildlife. There should also be a conscious effort to preserve the sanctity of those jungles. Often, tourists have been found littering and using plastics in areas high above those mountains. These can be dangerous for our environment. The Himalayas have always been equated with divinity in our culture. They are the Gods' abode, more pious than any man-made structure or building. Hence, we must not in any way cause harm to the flora and fauna of those places. Also, both these hamlets are easily accessible from most of the important cities in India through the Bagdogra Airport or the NJP Railway Junction. Therefore, the accessibility is quite modern. Let us now come to our conclusion. We can easily say that these two hamlets are two of the most beautiful places in India without a shadow of doubt. I hope their sublimity stays true to its nature forever.

Eight

THE LAND OF THE LAKES

We have discussed the Kumaon region of Uttarakhand as one of the two distinct zones of this state. Furthermore, the Kumaon jungles are inextricably linked to the memories of Jim Corbett, one of the greatest naturalists and hunters who once lived in these parts of British India. His most popular book till today is perhaps the 'Man-Eaters of Kumaon.' Stories from this book have been included, time and again, in several academic curricula in this country and in several compendiums. Therefore, right from our school days, we have been acquainted with the flora and fauna of this region. Just like the Garhwal part of Uttarakhand, Kumaon too has an interesting etymological backstory. As per legends, this was the place where one of the earliest incarnations of Lord Vishnu, another of the trinities of Hinduism, was born or took his shape and dwelled as the Kurma Avatar (Turtle/Tortoise in English). Hence, the name Kumaon eventually took its current shape from the word Kurma. Some of the most stunning hill stations in India are located in this region – viz., Nainital, Ranikhet, Kausani, Almora, Munsiyari, Chaukori, etc. The local people here are called Kumaoni, and they speak a language by the same name, which distinctly belongs to the Indo-Aryan (Indo-European) language family.

Nainital is the centre of this zone and also one of the most popular hill stations in India. The name Nainital has again been derived from the same legend of Hinduism that we saw in our earlier chapter. Nain, in the local tongue, means eyes. Goddess Sati's eyes are said to have fallen here, and *'tal'* means a body of water. Hence, Nainital is considered as one of the important Shakti Peethas of Hinduism. In this place, the north side of the lake has a Naina Devi Temple and the town has been developed around this water body. Nainital is also called the Lake District of Uttarakhand because it has several other gigantic and beautiful lakes in its vicinity – Naukuchiatal, Bhimtal, Sattal, etc. A hill station with such a huge lake is always an added attraction for many. That is why Nainital is a much sought-after place in comparison to the other hill stations of Northern India. But apart from its natural splendour, Kumaon is also historically very important in the context of this sub-continent. There are prehistoric cave paintings in this region which speak of the presence of the earliest human civilisations here. During the mediaeval ages too, the Katyuri Dynasty kings who ruled over this part also distinguished themselves with their administrative style and military might. After the British annexed Kumaon in the early 19th century, the hill station of Nainital was later founded when a sugar merchant by the name of Mr. P. Baron chanced upon this area while meandering through these hills during one of his hunting trips. While talking about hunters and hunting, it is important to note that at present, tourists can check out the two houses of Jim Corbett in Nainital. One is called "Gurney House" and is a private property now. The other bungalow is situated in a place called "Kaladhungi," which is located around 35 km away from Nainital town. This Kaladhungi house serves currently as a Jim Corbett museum.

In the spring of the year 2002, a friend took me to this beautiful region of Uttarakhand. The first thing that caught my eye en route was the lush greenery, which reminded us of the eerie settings of those Corbett stories. Those were pre-internet days and I was not aware of a place called Bhowali, close to Nainital, which housed Smt Kamala Nehru once. The wife of our first prime minister was treated there at the TB sanatorium for her ailment. It was one of the first things that my friend showed me there. For the next few days, we travelled the zone on his old Vespa scooter with unbridled enthusiasm. Tiredness was the last thing on our minds as we explored. A few kilometres before the town of Almora, we had once stopped at a place which was cemented with a canopy. Upon asking about the significance, a local *chaiwala* (tea vendor) told us a beautiful story. Once, when the great Indian monk Swami Vivekananda was travelling through the Kumaon Himalayas, he reached this place after a continuous walk of around 75 km. Before entering the town of Almora, exhaustion got the better of him, and he supposedly fainted right there. But a Muslim vendor found him in that perilous state, and he revived the monk by applying cucumber and water to his mouth. Ever since then, that spot has been revered as a place of great significance. The town of Almora is, of course, intrinsically connected today to the memories of that great monk. We kept on hearing innumerable stories and legends of the same kind as we travelled. But the crux of that tour was my ascent to the top of one of the peaks of Nainital. We shall come to that soon.

The other lakes and places that we travelled to and fro in that zone, showered an equal amount of serenity on our battered souls. When we sat on the shores of Naukuchiatal for hours on end, the gentle breeze from those immeasurable depths of water travelled to our weary bones just like a divine balm. At that moment, I was not aware of the religious significance of that body of water. The name Naukuchiatal means "a lake with nine bends" in the local language. Several travel magazines and blogs nowadays inform us that a visit to all those nine corners of the lake or a parikrama (circumambulation) of them brings moksha to the seeker. However, our time was spent during that trip taking in the natural splendour rather than the request for any spiritual solace, in that lake due to our ignorance then. Later on, this place also used to host a popular art and music festival, which has remained unattended by me till this moment. (Presently, with the ongoing pandemic, I am not even sure if that festival still takes place). Simultaneously, the other places that we travelled to, like the Jageshwar Temple complex or the Ranikhet golf course, brought an equal sense of calm and happiness.

Now, coming back to the vicinity of Nainital, let us first understand its topography. Once you reach the town, the first thing that comes to your notice is the gigantic lake flanked by three massive hilltops. Straight ahead from the north end of the lake is the Naina peak, also called the China peak since the local people there believe that our borders with Tibet are visible from that place. It is the highest point in Nainital. If you are facing the lake, on your left-hand side is the Tiffin Top, or Dorothy's Seat, and on your right-hand side is the snow view point, accessible through a rope-way (cable car). During that trip, my aim had been to trek up to the Tiffin Top, which is around 4 km from the lakeside. Tiffin Top is also called Dorothy's Seat. There is a love story behind this nomenclature. But when I visited it, a very different version of the story was narrated to me. In reality, the place was originally named after the wife of a British officer who wanted to honour his dead wife, killed en route on a voyage. But I was told that an English lady by that name had committed suicide from that point and hence the name. Never mind the story, the place looked quite eerie anyway during my trip.

On a certain afternoon during my aforementioned journey, I decided to take the Tiffin Top trek. I don't remember the exact date now. But it was a very sunny and bright afternoon. On an impulse, looking at the paucity of time, I had hired a pony too. The Tiffin Top trek is actually quite treacherous amidst thick foliage and a steep uphill climb. A guide is a must, hence. (I am just guessing that the route has remained the same at present). Therefore, the pony and its master acted more like a guide to me than a ride. Let me inform you here about this habit of the ponies. They would invariably take the edge of a mountainous route towards the abyss. Trust me, that is something which is really scary, and until and unless your breath has not given away totally because of the steep climb, it is always better to walk than to ride a pony on hills. Hence, I hired the man with his animals more as a backup for my trek. But that Pahari chap turned out to be quite an excellent raconteur. Unfortunately, I have completely forgotten his name now. Perhaps it was Raju or Shamu or something with the same sounding syllables. As we trudged up the hill, sometimes on foot and sometimes on the pony, we chatted a lot. My guide narrated a lot of stories about the local customs, food, festivals, and tourism of Kumaon. The distance did not feel daunting, and hence we took it slow. Once, when we had reached an even ground, the guide beckoned me to stop there. *"Sirji, do you remember this ground?"* he suddenly asked. After racking my brains for some time, I had to relent. I told him that I didn't quite understand what he was referring to. *"Sirji, don't you remember that famous song from that popular 80s movie? Where Mr. Shah was shown carrying his illegitimate son on his back? It was shot here."* Aah, I suddenly remembered that movie then, the debut film of a director who would later go on to achieve international acclaim. At another bend in the road, he again showed me an educational institute located amidst the hilly verdure at a stone's throw distance from that spot. *"Sirji, have you seen that academy? This was where the big man of Bollywood got educated. Many others too."* Though there was no way to check that trivia then, I took it at face value. He kept on pointing to me several other spots with filmy significance, but I don't remember them now. But the walk was one of a kind. The chirping of the birds all around seemed like the distant echo of a mellifluous thunder. The greenery was intoxicating with unknown smells emanating from the thick foliage. The weather remained beautiful with clear skies, though the perpetual fog was unmistakable. All that made the experience of an uphill climb quite refreshing. There is always something magical about the vegetation of the hills. The abundance of pine, deodar, oak, maple, and other trees seems heavenly. They embrace you in a knot of an unknown passion, seldom ephemeral but lingering for a very long time. Even today, the smell of that place is quite vivid in my mind. I can still feel the soothing mountain air and the gentle waves of the Naini Lake deep in my bosom. Like the flickering light of an eventful halogen, the memories keep coming back to me. When we finally reached the Tiffin Top, aka Dorothy's Seat, the all-encompassing views of the Kumaoni Mountains took my breath away. The tapestry of those undulating figures, with waves and waves of mountains and clouds, rolling on towards a never-ending horizon, was like an enchanting potion to the eyes. At that moment, I was overwhelmed with gratitude for both my guide and Mother Nature, who had created such bewildering sights and sounds for us, humanity. Again, I don't remember now the amount of time we spent there. But the approaching evening on the hills always made our sojourn shorter. Though the heart never agreed, I had to retreat after a point of time. But as said earlier, the vistas would linger even after my return to the hot plains of this sub-continent. On that trip, once we got back to our base, where my friend waited with bated breath with his ever-reliable Vespa scooter, my wanderings eventually came to their inevitable end. In spite of being a popular hill station, the peaks of Nainital were abashed with rumours of wildlife at that time. There were incidents when a certain village on the periphery encountered a leopard who came for their cows. Hence, the after-dark hours were never conducive to venturing outside, apart from commonplaces like a mall road or the main bazaar, etc. Maybe, the Tiffin Top peak also witnesses the apparition of that unfortunate Dorothy, whose memory reverberates in its nooks and crannies. During my hike, allusions were definitely made to me about the same. But then, nobody would wait until dark there to justify the truth behind this supposition.

However, all these short treks to the peaks of Nainital are worth the effort. They are not very strenuous and can be completed within a few hours. But a guide is a must on any hill. A good and trusted guide can also show you places that are not mentioned in any common brochure, travel guide books, or blogs. At the end of the day, we must conclude that Nainital is a beautiful place apart from all the constructions that have made the town quite congested now. But the discussed peaks, the lake, the surrounding mountains and all other places in its vicinity have given this hill station a very unique aura. There is no dearth of beautiful places in the Kumaon Himalayas. But an exploration of this region should be started with a visit to its epicentre, the most popular town in this zone. While in Nainital, one must never miss this short trek to the pinnacle of Dorothy's Seat, where the sky awaits with its colourful disposition to charm an intrepid traveller. Though a little bit of fitness and courage is required, not attempting that place will be a bigger miss. As the lines of a Hindi song from a 1999 movie truly convey – *"Taalon mein Nainital, Baaki sab talaiya,"* (roughly translates to – *There is no other lake like Nainital, the rest are just mere shallow water bodies*), this hill station is definitely the cynosure of all the places in Kumaon. A visit to this place should always be undertaken at least once a year or once in every three years.

Nine

Where The Lord Appeared
After His Vanishing Act

"*Angrez ne sher ko kaha mara tha?*" *(Where did the Englishman kill the tiger/leopard?)*

This question might sound odd to many. But anybody passing through the town of Rudraprayag today would definitely ask it. However, Corbett's iconic story 'The Man-Eating Leopard of Rudraprayag' has made this region popular amongst a global crowd long before modern tourism has taken its roots there. But anybody knowing the significance of a Prayag would still visit this place without learning or reading about the aforementioned account. For your information, in modern times, most of the local shop vendors and tea stall owners in the town still cannot identify Jim Corbett by his Christian name. (Well, they were not able to recognise the name during my visit). They only knew him as an English gentleman who had once killed a dreaded man-eater and made this place safer for the pilgrims. If you ask them on the spot by uttering the name of Corbett, they won't understand you. But the moment you say *Angrez* (Englishman), they will point you out that precise space marked by a plaque now honouring the famous killing of that dreaded man-eating leopard by Jim Corbett. (Sometimes, some local people also utter the name as 'Carpit Sahib'.)

The town of Rudraprayag is one of the most important junctions en route to two of the holiest shrines in Hinduism – Kedarnath and Badrinath. Even during the time of Corbett, this place was important in the context of the pilgrimages to the above two shrines. During the early part of the twentieth century, this area had once been tormented for some time by a man-eating leopard. After several attempts, the beast remained beyond the reach of humans. When Corbett was called for the task, rumours about the animal were ripe. Some informed the hunter that the leopard was actually a Tantric monk who could shape shift, making him impossible to kill or capture. By that time, since it had hunted scores of humans, people were also scared to their bones. If you read Jim Corbett's account of this leopard, you will know how he finally managed to kill it after much trial and tribulations. Today, when the pilgrims are journeying towards Kedarnath, a stop at this famous spot can be made. Prayag means confluence, and this town is a part of the famous Panch Prayag of Uttarakhand (*Panch* means five). The other four are Vishnuprayag, Karnaprayag, Nandaprayag, and Devprayag. In Rudraprayag, the river Mandakini, which flows down from the Kedarnath region, merges with the Alakananda and bustles ahead further down in full glory. This chapter deals with the divine Kedarnath shrine, and hence, Rudraprayag is an important cog in our journey.

The shrine of Kedarnath is an intrinsic part of the region of Uttarakhand. This land was once called "Kedarkhand" (people still refer to it by that name nowadays). The name Kedarnath more or less means the 'Lord of the Land.' For us Bengalis, the auteur Satyajit Ray's famous adventure story *"Ebaar Kando Kedarnathe"* (Adventures this time in Kedarnath) also inspired us towards this pious place right from our childhood. But before we proceed towards the narration of the Kedarnath Temple trek, let us first discuss its history and religious significance.

According to popular belief, the current temple of Shri Kedarnathji was built sometime in the eighth century CE at the behest of Shri Adi Shankaracharya. Adi Shankara was an Indian monk who promulgated the doctrine of Advaita Vedanta and thereby revived Hinduism, as per many historians. It is needless to mention here that Kedarnath is just another name for Lord Shiva. This shrine is a part of the Char Dham yatra of Uttarakhand. (Badrinath, Gangotri, and Yamunotri are the other three dhams.) This shrine is also a part of Panch Kedar, which we shall discuss soon. The other four shrines Panch Kedar are Tunganath, Rudranath, Madhyamaheshwar, and Kalpeshwar. Kedarnathji is also considered to be one of the most pious twelve Jyotirlingas of Lord Shiva in India.

The Kedarnath Shrine is now only open during the summer months for a limited time. The winter months experience heavy snowfall. Due to this, during those months, the idol of Lord Shiva is brought down to a place called Ukhimath, situated at a much lower altitude. Therefore, during the winter months, the idol of Lord Shiva is worshipped in Ukhimath. Out of the Panch Kedar Temples, Kedarnath Shrine is the most beautiful one. This is something that is universally accepted and, hence, it is also the most popular of all the places. The shrine is located at an elevation of nearly twelve thousand feet above sea level, and it is only accessible by foot after a 14-15/16 km hike from a place called Gaurikund.(As we already know, Gauri is another name for Lord Shiva's consort).

Now, coming back to the legend of the creation of Panch Kedar, perhaps in Uttarakhand there is seldom any place not connected to the events narrated in the Indian epic of

'Mahabharata.' Therefore, Panch Kedar shrines are also believed to have been built by the Pandava brothers. The story goes like this: After the dreaded Kurukshetra War, where savagery reached an extreme pinnacle, the Pandavas were crestfallen by that wanton bloodshed. Since the perpetrators were themselves, the conscience hit them hard after they had annihilated almost all their relatives. Therefore, they wanted to atone for their sins, and with that desire in their hearts, they reached the holy abode of Kashi (Banaras/Varanasi, presently) to seek Lord Shiva's blessings. By that time, Lord Shiva had grown quite disappointed in them. After all, who would support such killings on a massive scale? Hence, in order to avoid them, the great god turned himself into a bull and then hid himself in a place called Guptkashi. Today, Guptkashi falls in the way when you are driving towards Gaurikund. This place got its name as per the above story. (*Gupt* means hidden in Hindi). But according to the same legend, the Pandavas, being smart, found the Lord in that place soon. He was probably spotted by his second brother, Bhima. Therefore, the Lord dived into the ground and the hump part of his bull form appeared in Kedarnath (hence the shape of the idol there). The Lord's other body parts simultaneously appeared in the rest of the four places – Tunganath, Rudranath, Madhyamaheshwar, and Kalpeshwar. Hence, in order to appease the great god, the Pandavas then built five temples in those places and worshipped him. In that way, they absolved themselves of the terrible sins that they had committed earlier. Thus, it is believed that the original Panch Kedar shrines were built by the Pandava brothers. For the record, all these five shrines are located amidst the Himalayan splendour and are extremely beautiful in their own ways even today. During the month of October in the year 2001, I made a solo trip to that heaven.

At the beginning of this new millennium, I was a student in Dehradun. Those were the days before social media. Though the use of the internet had started by then, its proliferation was still a few days away. Therefore, the flow of information was moved mostly by words of mouth, and some by the extensive reading of newspapers, magazines, or books. But I was always a well-informed man. From different sources, I had read about Kedarnath Dham already by then. My mountain spirit was just hankering for a moment to take the trip. Therefore, one October morning, without thinking about it too much, I packed my bag and went ahead. After getting up very early in the morning and drinking a cup of tea served by my landlady, I went straight to the bus stand. Upon reaching there, a chance discovery got me into a trekker jeep which was ferrying passengers till Rudraprayag on a sharing basis. Instead of travelling by a rugged general bus for ten or twelve hours straight to Gaurikund, I found the option of a break-journey through multiple stops a much better option. Therefore, the decision to use that jeep did not take much time. As the open-roofed vehicle plodded towards its destination, the morning rays of a gentle sun glided into our expectant eyes. The morning highway turned a pleasant hue, as always. (Much deforestation has happened ever since on the Dehradun-Rishikesh road). Slowly but gradually, our vehicle left the scorching plains and meandered through a mountainous pathway. My heart leapt with joy when the jeep passed through Devprayag. It is the place where the mighty Alakananda merges with Bhagirathi and thereby flows as the holy Ganga towards the plains. From there, it did not take us much time to reach the old capital of Garhwal – Srinagar (not the one in Kashmir). We did not stop there and eventually reached Rudraprayag. After a sumptuous brunch, I took another trekker jeep to the next destination on that route – Guptkashi. The same course of action was taken until the most crucial point of the journey. By evening, I finally reached Gaurikund and took a fine room in a hotel. The place was teeming with pilgrims and tourists. Remember, the year was 2001 and the place was a bustling centre from where the trek to the Kedarnath Shrine started. Therefore, I found many hotels and eateries there, and the hot springs were converted into a huge giant public bathing system at the centre of that location for the devotees. In Hinduism, Gaurikund is a place of special significance. This was supposed to be the spot where Devi Gauri meditated and prayed, and hence received the Great Lord Shiva as her devout husband. This was also the site where Lord Ganesha, their son, mistakenly lost his original head and was finally restored with the head of an elephant that we now see and worship. However, during my stay there I did not take a dip in that pious water, being shy and lazy, but roamed around and observed the pilgrims. There were people of all ages, nationalities, and types. It was really a motley crew of quite an extraordinary kind. The place was abuzz with their chanting and a certain energy flowed there that made all my tiredness go away in a jiffy. Nevertheless, eventually, I had to retreat and have my dinner early. The plan for the next day was to start the trek before 4.30 am in the early morning. Here, I must mention something about that special dinner. To my utter delight, I found a hotel with Bengali cuisine. They served me an extraordinary *'thali'* with their modest means. The pure veg food tasted nothing less than an elixir. As I gulped a fair amount of ghee together with rice, lentils, and other vegetables, the full tummy soon made my eyes droopy. Soon, the hotel bed beckoned as I retired to my hearth for that night.

Some magic mechanism hitherto unfathomed, made me wake up sharp at 4 am the next morning. Within the next half hour, I was ready, after a bath, to go to perhaps one of the most beautiful places on this earth. As scores of pilgrims took to the road for the hike up, I followed them, with a stick in my hand and all alone. But the road soon found me making companions after companions. We all felt like we were part of the same family, treading towards a divine pathway, seeking the eternal truth. The energy flowing through our veins was kind of mesmerizing. We were shivering with excitement. It was not just a trek, but a journey into life's most enthralling realisations. The surroundings appeared to my eyes as the meadows of a pristine Garden of Eden. Mountains after mountains sang to me with their effervescence and magical tunes. The rolling green valleys swathed in that morning's dews glinted like a million diamonds on display. As we trudged ahead, people from the opposite side, who were returning by then, shouted at us with phrases like "Har Har Mahadev", "Jai Bhole Baba" (Hail to the Great Lord), thereby inspiring us to go ahead with equal gusto. The pilgrims on that pathway were encouraging each other all the time. After all, for a general human being from the plains of India, the distance was not an easy one to cover. But it was worth the effort anyhow. The experience was mind-blowing and something to not miss at all. There were also stoppages in the hike, and shops at certain bends where we got coffee, Maggie, and other snacks. After replenishing ourselves thus, we finally reached the settlement of the Kedarnathji Dham at around high noon. As soon as the spire of the shrine came into my view from a distance, I felt as if I was entering a very ancient place. The mountains all around us looked like sentries from the era of the Mahabharata. After all, this was the site where the Pandavas once made their offerings to the Great Lord Shiva. Yes, I was entering the same heaven. A place steeped in history and heritage. A matter of faith but also of feelings. After reaching the settlement, a beautiful *dharamshala* (rest house) took me as their guest. The place served me hot water and then a nice meal. After getting refreshed, thus, I took to my heels and explored the surroundings. It is needless to mention here the splendour of the architecture of the Kedarnath Temple, the beautiful intricacy of its curvature and design, how imposing the structure looked during my time and still is. There have been scores of writers, poets, scribes, and travellers who have quite effusively described this gorgeous and magnificent shrine all over these years. Behind the temple, the white peaks shone dazzlingly in the setting sun of that day. Some people also showed me the supposed Samadhi Staal of Adi Shankaracharya, situated behind the temple at a short distance. The hours passed in a blink. The night-time had a limited power supply. Hence, I again retired to my bed quite early that evening. The next dawn saw me getting up early again at around 4-5 am. As I looked outside my hotel windows, the last rays of the moon and then the first sun rays of the morning, made the shrine awash with colours of multiple hues and shades of dazzling beauty. What a sight it was! (And what a sight it must be now, and will always be.) The day saw me making an entry to the temple, worshipping there and then exploring the surroundings. A venture to the high-up lake was abandoned soon after a failed attempt, which was made foolishly without a guide. As the hours passed quickly, the time also came to make the descent back to Gaurikund. By that time, the Kedarnath Dham got choc-a-bloc with both foreign and domestic tourists. After some time, I checked out of my rest house and started my return journey. Again, it is needless to mention here that the return downhill trek was quite easy in comparison and I reached Gaurikund in much lesser time. From Gaurikund, I headed straight back to my original destination. There was no point in further waiting for anything, though I could have explored the surroundings a bit more. But being a student, the pressure of classes starting was making me constantly worried.

While in Kedarnath, I met a lot of tourists from my native place of Bengal. Many had already visited the shrine multiple times by then. Some even told me that during an earlier time, the priests of Kedarnathji knew a secret route which took them directly to Badrinath Dham without any hassle. They used to shift regularly between these two famous shrines, where they served as priests. Of course, these legends can never be proved without further shreds of evidence. During that time, I also found adequate supplies near the shrine - hotels, eateries, shops, etc. It was the month of October and hence quite cold for me. In fact, deep into the night, the chill was quite numbing but not something that was intolerable. Ever since then, the beautiful shrine of Kedarnath has remained very vivid in my memories. Though I was all alone on that trip, my solo meanderings had never encountered even a single hassle from any place on that sojourn. Well, there is no dearth of beautiful places in the Indian Himalayas. But out of them, Kedarnathji Shrine should be placed right on top. Om Naamo Shivay!

(Note: In the recent years, Kedarnath Shrine's facilities have become more developed than the time when I visited, I have been told. On mountains, things also change due to the climate and geography all the time. Hence, it is advisable that people must check the current data, rules and regulations before embarking upon a destination).

Ten

WHERE THE DESCENDANTS OF THE KURUKSHETRA WARRIORS RESIDE TODAY

Jaunsaris and Bawaris – we can say with some certainty that not many people in today's India have heard about these two very interesting clans. They live in the Jaunsar-Bawar region of the state of Uttarakhand. But the most intriguing part about them is that these two clans claim their descent (with much confidence and surety), directly from the Pandavas and the Kauravas of the epic Mahabharata. As we have discussed so many times earlier, we can see how the Mahabharata, created by Ved Vyas, is ubiquitous in the lives of most Indians, even in modern times. The state of Uttarakhand, which is so intrinsically connected to the religion of Hinduism, also has a special place for many events narrated in that epic. Therefore, it is not at all surprising that a group of people who live there claim their origins right from the heroes of Vyas's work. But hold on, why are we discussing them here? Because in that beautiful region of Jaunsar-Bawar, there is a hill station, which is one of the most serene places in India. The name of this hill retreat is Chakrata, and it has remained outside the cacophony of general tourism till now. This cantonment town is another of those places developed by the British during their rule to escape the terrible summer heat of the sub-continent.

Today, the place is a three-hour drive (well, almost) from the city of Dehradun, the capital of Uttarakhand. Chakrata sounds like a common enough name here in India, though its meaning is not clear to us as yet. The town is situated at an altitude of around 7000 ft. above sea level and, with its lush green settings, receives a fair amount of snowfall. This story is about my journey to that place during my student days. The autumn of the year two thousand came to us like a harbinger of good times. Unlike the West, where spring is celebrated in full glory, autumn in India is the best time to travel, or the best time for partying and bonhomie. The period experiences the first cool air of the season; slowly but surely, the scorching heat gives way to mild rays of an overheated sun above. One can experience a distinct flavour in the morning dew or a melancholy stupor in the evening sun that eventually goes away with the passing of cooler hours. After many months of hot, humid summer and then incessant rain, autumn brings a tolerable atmosphere to the people of this subcontinent. In the year two thousand (2000CE), I had just started as a student in the Doon Valley. To my utter delight, I also found two juniors at that time who were travel freaks like me. The pressure of study was quite numbing for all three of us. But that did not deter us from making a plan and visiting a most quaint and quiet place. A hill station already bloomed with the air of an autumnal breeze. Yes, we travelled to the cantonment town of Chakrata. But before we move on with the description of that place, I would like to narrate a personal account here. I hope it doesn't sound too boring to our readers. Long before the three of us made any plans for that place, I was experiencing a strange dream. All three of us at that time had been staying at a local paying-guest house. We had separate rooms for ourselves. My two juniors were called Kavi and Ananda by the other students.

Now, coming back to that private strange incident, in those months, on every night my dreams would take me to an unknown valley. There, the local people would treat me to some nice delicacies. But soon, I saw a woman there. A happy lassie with sea-wave eyelashes beckons me to go with her. But in my excitement, I slipped on the edge of the mountain and found myself rolling down the abyss in a continuous fall. That horrible dream came to me on numerous nights. But I could never make any head or tail of it. Those were days when my cravings for mountains hadn't really developed the way they are now. Before that trip, the only places that I had been to were Mussoorie and the hill stations of North-East India, where I belonged. Therefore, when Kavi, one of the juniors in my mess, made a plan for the three of us to travel to Chakrata, I was a bit sceptical. Indians are generally very superstitious about their dreams, and I was (and still am) no exception. But both Kavi and Ananda could convince me in the end. Being in my early twenties, that was also a time for me to dream about a companion. But why would a sweet dream of a lassie be followed by an accident? That ominous vision could only have been deciphered by a shrink. But anyway, now I am digressing. The purpose of bringing up this story of my dream is to make the readers understand how sceptical I was at that time about travelling to a new place.

Eventually, the three of us got ready. Being students, expenses were a priority with limited pocket money at that time. Hence, we got up at 3 am on the day of our journey to catch a trekker jeep that ferried passengers on a shared basis. (That was the best option at that time). When we got one at around 4 am, the daylight had not yet emerged. Being half-asleep, we still enjoyed the journey, which was quite smooth. When the sun finally came out, we had left the plains by then and meandered through the thick foliage of Himalayan outgrowth. The winding roads looked lush green after a heavy monsoon. My two juniors were gaping outside with their wide eyes. One of them, Kavi, had been to the hills before but not Ananda, the other kid. He was a complete novice who hadn't much travelled in the mountains of India. When we finally reached there, we could seek out decent accommodation in the form of a new hotel. At this moment, I don't exactly remember its name. But we found it located right at the heart of that small place. After we freshened up and had a hearty meal, the lodge manager suggested we visit the famous Tiger Falls of Chakrata. He probably suggested it looking at the fact that all three of us were young and hence capable of undertaking a small trek. At that moment, we learnt that the hike would be around 5 km one way, a fact later confirmed by various sources. But the onward journey turned out to be easy for us, as we had to climb down the mountain to reach that waterfall. So, the return trek of 5 km up the mountain would be tough, as we instantly realised at that moment.

However, in any case, the moment we left the town centre and took a jungle route for our hike, the gentle rays of the sun, along with the cool breeze of the mountain, took all our stress away. As we climbed down through those walkways of coniferous trees, at certain bends, we also met people from the local villages. However, we did not stop as reaching the waterfall was too exciting a prospect to wait. After a certain amount of time, we reached that sprouting water delight. The place looked wonderful, and because it was empty, we wasted no time in taking a plunge into that pool. The Tiger Waterfall felt wonderful to our eager souls. The surroundings again looked lush and green, with jungles embracing the place like a careful guardian. But nobody around that area could tell us the origin of the name.

However, looking at the surrounding jungles, we guessed that this waterfall must have been infested with leopards or maybe tigers at a certain point in time. But anyway, we had fun exploring the place and also playing with the water. We stood inside the plunging water for a long time, sometimes coming out and at other times going in. The water felt heavy on the shoulders after a few seconds. Therefore, we kept on changing places. Eventually, the time came when we had to leave the place. As we started the uphill trek, realisation dawned on the necessity of fitness. But we were young and Kavi, especially among the three of us, was super fit. While yours truly and Ananda huffed and puffed as we climbed, Kavi made it look very easy. We also had a lovely experience during the course of that trek. Once, when we passed a hut and decided to take a rest for some time near it, the owner of that dwelling, a local villager, offered us food. The kindness of that simple hilly man stunned us to no end. There was this man, barely able to sustain himself and his family in that difficult, rugged terrain. But he was as kind as divinity. In fact, most of the villagers that we met en route were very innocent. They had never even heard about television or railways at that time, a far cry from our fake modern world. After meeting such people and feeling good, the uphill climb became a little less tiresome.

The day soon turned into an impending twilight period. As the final rays of the setting sun converted the world into a tapestry of changing colours, we reached the flat ground from where our downhill climb started. From there, the town centre of Chakrata would have taken very little time. Therefore, without any further worries, all three of us then sat down there to take a breather and as we diverted our gauge towards the gorge from whence we reappeared, a breath-taking scene unfolded. We could see the snow peaks in the fading light of that evening, a shimmering apparition like presence, slight but distinct. Kavi gave a shout of joy and said that our journey had finally achieved its ultimate pinnacle. We kept on resting at that place before it finally became very dark and hence unsafe due to the jungle all around. We came back to our hotel in unabashed joy. The trip to this place turned out to be a very good exploration for us. The next day, we wandered through the various points of that cantonment zone and realised once again how peaceful it was. The local people also assured us of enough snowfall if we come in the winter. As alluded to earlier, the local folks there turned out to be extremely hospitable, and whether there was a Mahabharata connection or not, they also looked brave and bold to us.

Now for some general information. Chakrata, being an army zone, is not always open to foreigners. Strictly speaking, post-COVID rules are not very familiar to me at this moment or to any of my Doon friends there, as they keep on changing from time to time. The best thing would be to check with the local authorities there through the Uttarakhand administrative website. Not only the aforementioned Tiger Falls, but Chakrata also has other attractions too for any intrepid traveller from the plains. Not only me, but most of the people who have visited this place have also talked in glowing terms about the beauty and serenity of this hill station. The best way to reach this place is through the state capital of Dehradun. In fact, Mussoorie is also not far away from this lesser-known hill retreat. But to everybody, Chakrata will be a very good experience. For that Tiger Waterfall, there must be an alternative but less exhaustive route today. Things have surely changed quite a bit from the time of my visit to that exotic heaven.

Eleven

THE SACRIFICIAL LAND OF THE AVIFAUNA

As I sit down now to write this chapter, my heart aches to write anything. The beautiful place that I once visited in the year 1999 has now been devastated by a flood at this moment. As those tragic photos of the suffering of humans and nature keep on appearing on social media, the anguish increases with each moment. But we still haven't completely lost hope yet. We know about the resilience of the people in our hills. Natural calamities cannot break them easily, as they have proved time and again. For your information, this location is in Assam, where the rains lashed with ferocity in the summer of 2022, submerging many areas under its raging waters. We are talking about the Dima Hasaon hilly district of Assam, which includes Halflong and Jatinga, two of the most beautiful places in North-East India. You can also consider them a single place, as Jatinga is just a small village located on the outskirts of Halflong. Some people consider Halflong the only hill station in the state of Assam. When yours truly was a college student, along with my family, cousins, and friends, we travelled to this region in the summer of 1999. At that time, my fiction reading consisted mostly of the novels of the great Bengali authors. As a result, in one of the children's novels by the maestro Sunil Gangopadhyay, we learnt about Jatinga and about the beauty and mystery of that zone. Hence, the longing for this place was always there. Thankfully, one of our relatives has his native place situated in the town of Halflong. Therefore, when we travelled there in 1999, we stayed at his place. He and his family still reside in that small town. During our 1999 trip, he was the one who took us to every nook and cranny of that region. Hence, when we travelled down to the beautiful valley of Jatinga from his house, we did a bit of hiking. We drove down from the main road to the bustling stream flowing on the Jatinga riverbed below, braving the boulders and having a great time. This chapter is about the beautiful journey to that place and the exhilarating sights and sounds experienced there by us.

After reaching our relative's place and settling down in the summer of that year, we did not waste any time going outdoors and exploring the area. Therefore, one morning, on our constant plodding, a jeep hired by that relative took us to the outskirts of Halflong, towards Jatinga Valley, a few kilometres away. When we started our journey, the morning mist gave us a shivering chill down to our bones, as the jeep winded through those hilly terrains forever engulfed in clouds. At certain bends in that road, the clouds even entered our vehicle and created an aura of mystery and supernatural hues. At the same time, all around us, we found the surrounding mountains to be daunting.

Let me inform you here that we used to live in the Barak Valley of Assam in our childhood. From one of its towns, the hazy outline of these mountains was visible during the day, and hence we felt awed by their presence all the time. The district of Dima Hasao was known earlier as North Cachar Hills. At this moment, the region is home to many indigenous tribal groups, viz., the eponymous Dimasa, Kuki, Naga, etc. Almost all of them speak the Tibeto-Burman language. These hills of Dima Hasao are part of the Borail Range. Now, this Borail Range is a part of the Purvanchal Mountains, which are considered the eastern extreme of the Himalayan Range. During our travels then, before venturing into the Jatinga Valley, we had also visited other distinctive sites of interest in that town. Some of those are the local Kali Bari – the temple of the Mother Goddess in her warrior avatar, the Halflong Lake, where we rowed and had a wonderful relaxing time, the Halflong Circuit House, which serves as a viewpoint, etc. After completing all these, we journeyed to the most thrilling spot in that region. When we drove down to Jatinga, a moment came when our jeep finally reached a point in the road from where the valley appeared clearly to the eyes of the tourists with all its verdant rolling greens. Therefore, we decided to disembark there from that vehicle and trek down to the stream below on the bed of that gorge. Hence, as we braved the boulders and got down to the stream eventually, the surroundings looked ethereal. Not only had we carried food too, to have a picnic in that place, but the chilling water of the stream also did not deter us from taking a plunge as and when we found small pools to our liking. The resultant chill received from those baths thankfully did not make anybody ill. The stream, with its mild gurgling sound, soothed all the weary souls in our group. From that place, the phenomenon of the famous bird suicide of Jatinga also did not appear in our minds. Although, that ghastly matter of the mysterious demeanour of the birds had made everybody curious about the place before a sound scientific explanation came to knowledge, we had forgotten the same during our picnic. Now, let us discuss that matter. For an international audience, the attraction of the Jatinga Valley is due to the mystery of the migratory birds going there to commit suicide. Yes, you have heard that right. This story, presented in a children's novel as mentioned above, initially made my family and friends extremely interested to visit that place. However, as proved now, the birds there don't commit any suicide, but they still run to their annihilation. As they go there, the local villagers hunt them easily and then consume them with utter relish for their meals. But that is where the suspense still lies. Why would any bird fly just like a possessed creature to this valley just to get killed? We have to discuss the scientific explanation in detail behind that phenomenon. Now, let us take into account a certain period every year. In all probability, the time period of late August to early October, after the monsoon makes the atmosphere hazy there with further clouds, Therefore, when an evening turns dark in the Jatinga Valley with no moon during that period, with a certain direction of the wind after the rains, a certain number of birds rush to this valley when they see the illuminating spherical light cones perched on poles. These lights are being lit up by the villagers there to lure those birds. As a result, when those creatures fly towards those lights, the waiting villagers in that place catch them with ease and then cook their meat for a sumptuous dinner. But these birds are local and not migratory as per the popular grapevine. These local birds are also not nocturnal, and since they venture forth during their general resting hours, this odd behaviour has created a mystery in the minds of many experts. Thankfully, the authorities have now taken steps to make the local villagers desist from such killings. Further research is going on to ascertain this behaviour of the birds, but an accurate theory is still awaited. Many scientists, in the meantime, have proposed this logic: that the earth's magnetism in this valley affects in some way the central nervous systems of some local birds there. Due to this, they rush there during a certain pattern of the weather, and, in the process, fall prey to the hunting population there.

However, whatever the reason behind the mysterious behaviour of these birds, we hope that their killings won't happen again in the future, as the avifauna is as important to the well-being of this region as other factors. More so, as we have recently seen, climate change can easily devastate a specific zone. All the places in this region, like Halflong, Jatinga, Harangajao, Mahur, Maibong, etc., and the rest of the Barail Range Mountains are ecologically and environmentally extremely sensitive. Therefore, all efforts should be made to maintain the greenery there and to preserve its inhabitants. Halflong can be easily reached either from Silchar with its airport or from a town called Lumding, situated to the south-east of Guwahati. In the near future, we hope to see this place full of its earlier glory and rehabilitated with its original scenery again.

Till then, our prayers are always with the local people of Dima Hasao.

Twelve

CONCLUSION

This book is based on this age-old adage: "That if you don't take to the roads on your feet in this country, you won't be able to see the real India." As a result, the journeys described here are only possible through the exertion of one's own limbs. Most of these places can also be visited on horseback. Moreover, nowadays, in the majority of these regions, alternative means have also come up (or are coming up at the time of writing this piece) for enabling easy travel to these spots. So, ultimately, it depends on the choice of an individual traveller whether he or she would like to hike or take an easy way out. If you ask me, the real fun lies in walking and hiking.

Further, the readers must have noticed in the previous chapters that all the travels mentioned in this work are quite simple treks. They don't have great elements of risks, as such. Of course, even a short trek on a mountain requires some amount of physical exertion and some amount of safety. Therefore, some basic fitness is required to attempt any place that can be reached only through a hike. But personally speaking, I have never been a fan of strenuous trekking or even mountaineering. These are for professionals and require certain parameters of conditioning and preparation. The risk involved is also high, and the loss of lives is also one of the eventualities. But more than the fear of the loss of innocent lives, what I detest about all these serious mountaineering expeditions is the disturbance they cause to the natural habitats of flora and fauna. Call me a puritan or old-fashioned, but I sincerely believe that the deep core of a mountain is not meant for humans. The summits of those peaks are not meant for us. They are the abodes of gods and goddesses. By divinity here, I also mean nature, which is too beautiful there to be disturbed with the traces of our dirty feet. Let us leave the mountains as they are. There is no need to explore all the summits. To test our endurance against the harshness of nature is just an exercise in ego massaging, and nothing else. We are too minuscule for nature. Let us not invite her wrath. It is a well-known fact that wherever humans have set foot, they have only destroyed the sublimely natural beauty of a place.

The preceding chapters, as you have noticed, are also narrated chronologically from the most recent to the most distant past ones. This has been done keeping in mind the relevance of the features of a place. In the mountains of India, as in anywhere else, things keep on changing. New roads or thoroughfares have come up in most places. Some geographical changes have also occurred due to earthquakes or other factors. Also, most of the areas have undergone massive deforestation in all these years. A population explosion is a major cause of environmental problems in this subcontinent. As the cities have become overcrowded, people are now taking over the jungles and the mountains. With each passing day, environmental degradation continues. The encroachment of humans has also severely harmed ecological balance. All this may sound very pessimistic. But we still have time if we become conscious. A beautiful country like India requires utmost care and love. This country has no dearth of beautiful places. Along with its human and cultural diversity, it also has infinite biodiversity. We need to wake up before it is too late. The biodiversity of this country is its greatest asset. It has to be preserved. Let me finish this piece with a couple of immortal lines from this iconic poem by the poet Iqbal:

Saarey Jahaan Se Achchaa,
Hindustan Hamaraa Hamaraa, Hum Bul Bulain Hai Iss Ki,
Ye Gulsitan Hamaraa Hamaraa.

Acknowledgements

When it comes to mountains, there are no dearth of books and there are no dearth of stories. Therefore, naturally, I have been much inspired to travel in the mountains all my life by reading works of greats like Ruskin Bond, Satyajit Ray (Many of Ray's detective stories are based on hill stations), Bibhutibhushan Bandopadhyay, Stephen Alter, Bill Bryson, and many such geniuses like them. For this book, I would specially like to thank my family, my friends, my guides in my travels, all those hotel managers who have been extremely helpful, my editors and publisher and various other known and unknown people. I would also like to point out that any mistake made in this book is purely my fault. I sincerely hope that the readers would pardon the gaffes and the slips and would enjoy it as an engrossing travelogue. May God bless us always and keep our country beautiful, happy and prosperous.

ABOUT THE AUTHOR

Saurav Ranjan Datta is an Indian author and columnist known for his works on history, travel, and real-life-inspired stories. He has written many articles for several national and international publications, like the Hindustan Times, CNBCTV18, Timeless Travels Magazine UK, Outlook India, Times Journal, The Statesman Kolkata, Kitaab.org, Ancient Origins Magazine, Ancient History Encyclopedia, Sulekha.com, Firedeye.com, Utkal Today, The Assam Tribune, HT OTT, Moorshead History Magazine, and The Indian Hour. He has also written poems and short stories for several other anthologies and publishers. His first book, "Maidens of Fate," is based on real-life incidents that the author encountered in his early years. His second book, Where Bravehearts Dwelt, is based on Indian history. The genre is historical fiction. He has written it with the purpose of presenting history in an interesting way to young people. His third book, "Goddesses of Fury: History's Most Daring Queens," is a purely non-fictional work on history. Several academic bodies have mentioned and referenced it. Many Wikipedia articles have also taken this book as their reference point.

Are you an aspiring writer looking for a publisher?

Let Team Simplicité serve you. Manuscripts invited.
Mail your proposal at livesimplicite@ gmail.com

We are traditional publishers and publish fiction, non-fiction, poetry and academic books in English language. To know more, DM @ livesimplicite on Instagram, Facebook and Twitter.

9 789358 986938